"SOAR, EAT ETHER, SEE WHAT HAS NEVER BEEN SEEN;
DEPART, BE LOST, BUT CLIMB."

—EDNA ST. VINCENT MILLAY

D1596987

REVOLUTIONARY
RECUITING

HOW THE FAREMOUTH METHOD HELPS
JOB SEEKERS, RECRUITERS, AND BUSINESSES
LEARN TO MATCH PEOPLE WITH THEIR PASSIONS

MARY ANN FAREMOUTH

NORTH STAR ATHENA
PUBLISHING LLC

Published by North Star Athena Publishing LLC, Houston, Texas

Copyright © 2017 Mary Ann Faremouth.

For more info, please visit www.faremouth.com, or email the author at faremouth@sbcglobal.net.

Content/Developmental Editing by Max Regan
Line Editing / Proofreading by D Tinker Editing
Cover Design and Book Layout by MarkGelotte.com

Library of Congress Control Number: 2017905752

ISBN-13: 978-0-9988658-1-2

25 24 23 22 21 20 19 18 17   1 2 3 4 5

TO MY LATE HUSBAND, BOB SANDLAND,

WHO IS THE WIND BENEATH MY WINGS.

CONTENTS

INTRODUCTION .... I X

Chapter 1
MAKING THE MATCH.. 1

Chapter 2
BUSINESS AS USUAL...17

Chapter 3
THE FAREMOUTH METHOD.................................... 3 2

Chapter 4
FOR THE RECRUITER.. 4 5

Chapter 5
FOR THE JOB SEEKER 77

Chapter 6
FOR THE EMPLOYER..118

Chapter 7
HUMAN TO HUMAN... 142

ACKNOWLEDGMENTS 151

REFERENCES..155

INTRODUCTION

In 2001, my husband died of a broken heart. Tall, dark, handsome, and intelligent, he was a mechanical engineer with a degree from Texas A&M University. He was a fourth-generation Houstonian, loved to hunt and fish, and became an Eagle Scout at age seventeen. His dream in life was to become a forest ranger. When he entered college, his parents suggested that he pursue an engineering degree, like his father and uncle before him. They believed that such a career path would afford him the kind of affluent life they thought he would enjoy. After two years of struggling with mechanical engineering courses, he tried to change his major to forestry, but in the end he chose to stay on his career path. After he graduated, he took a job with International Paper and moved away to North Carolina, beginning his career as a mechanical engineer.

After many years, he came home to Houston to work in the family business as a technical sales engineer. We went on one blind date and married nine months later. I remember how miserable my husband was in his job and all the times he would come home early from work with severe migraine headaches. As a professional recruiter focused on making a good match for my clients, I soon discovered that my husband was in the wrong job.

On April 18, 1995, the *Houston Post* closed. Its assets and liabilities were acquired by Hearst Corporation, the publisher of the *Houston Chronicle*. When this happened, my husband suggested we try to create an employment publication. At the time, I was self-employed as an independent recruiter and extremely busy. But I knew that my husband was unhappy in his career. Plus, he had a knack for serving others and was good with graphic design. It was a far cry from forestry, but I could see that this project would give him an outlet for his natural talents and abilities. I had experience in the employment world, so between the two of us I felt we could give it a whirl. What really motivated me, however, was seeing the way my husband lit up every time he talked about the project!

We bought a cheap phone from RadioShack, we hired a PR firm to design a logo, and the publication *Jobs: Houston* was ready to launch. In the first six months, I was the only salesperson. My husband wrote the articles and handled page layout. We published the paper every two weeks. In a very short time, we had full-page ads from many large, reputable companies, and as time went on, we grew to sixteen employees and a full-time graphic designer and we hosted many job fairs. But as busy as we were, my husband was still working two full-time, very stressful jobs. He would work most days in his technical sales job with the family business and would only come to work at the *Jobs: Houston* office late in the afternoon. Looking back, I believe he was being pulled in two directions—between the work he truly loved and the work he was committed to doing.

And then one day, our world was turned completely upside down. My husband was in my office when he complained of severe pain in his neck. A few days later, at only forty-seven years old, he died of a dissecting aneurism—a severe medical condition in which the middle and inner layers of the aorta separate. His heart had essentially split in two. After his death, I was consumed by shock and grief, even as I was faced with maintaining our business and raising two children alone. Eventually, I sold *Jobs: Houston* magazine to a well-known, successful publishing company and went back to my recruiting firm full-time. But I was haunted by the divided heart that had created so much of my husband's stress and ultimately led to his death.

Two years ago, a young man named Jason was referred to me. Jason had a degree in forestry and had been looking for a job for a year without any success. His life had changed significantly since he received his degree, and he wanted a new career in the oil and gas industry. When he told me his background, I was stunned; his story was the mirror opposite of my husband's career.

I was determined to place him in a job that would utilize his skills, abilities, and passions and bring him career satisfaction. Jason was a special young man, and I took the time to dig deep into his background to find out who he was and what his interests were. I discovered he had a strong math and science background, he liked to move around in his job instead of just sitting behind a desk, and he was so skilled with computers that he could practically make them sing and dance. At the time, I had a job listing for a production coordinator in a manufacturing plant, but this young man had almost none of the traditional requirements on his resume. In fact, I believe that ninety-nine out of a hundred recruiters would have overlooked him. But what the job actually required was a person who could synthesize technical data and interface with the other departments. It needed someone who could maintain quality, environmental, and safety regulations and put all the data into complex Excel spreadsheets. The company was reluctant to interview him, but when they did, he was hired on the spot. His passions and commitments were perfectly aligned with the job. Within thirty days, Jason had been promoted, and in his time with the company, he has been promoted an additional three times. He is now the proud father of two beautiful children, enjoys a lucrative career, and has told me he is very happy.

My work with Jason made me realize how many millions of people have careers that are not aligned with their passions and personalities. And my experience in losing my beloved husband made me eternally aware of the long-term price of being miserable in your job. The Faremouth Method—the series of steps I used to place Jason and hundreds of other job seekers into jobs that align with their passions, skills, and abilities—can help applicants, recruiters, and businesses match people with the jobs of their dreams.

Staying true to the core of what gives us joy can lead us to career paths that more strongly match who we really are.

CHAPTER 1
MAKING THE MATCH

Why the Wrong Person Might Be Right for the Job

I've been an executive recruiter for over thirty years now, and most people would never believe just how often I have placed the wrong person (or so they look on paper) into the perfect job. In my practice, I look behind and beyond the resume to align the whole person with the job. Initially, a lot of people who call the shots in the businesses that hire me thought this approach sounded crazy. They were content to scan applicants' resumes for the same old information, ticking off boxes for the right job experience, the right educational degrees in the right fields, and the right keywords. Then they wondered why their "right" hires didn't even last the month.

But when many of them failed to find, hire, or retain the right people to fill the job, they came to me, finally willing to try the method that has been the core of my business from the beginning. And they weren't disappointed.

The Faremouth Method

The Faremouth Method consists of the following five steps, each of which is enacted differently by prospective job seekers, employers, and recruiters. Here are the basics:

I. *Do a Self-Inventory*
   A self-inventory is the first, most vital step in the journey a business or an individual takes toward making the right employment match. This is where you will find out who you truly are, what you care about, what your values are, and what you truly want. This inventory takes time, but it gives you the key information you need to get on the right path.

2. *Ask Better Questions*
   In this step, recruiters, applicants, and businesses learn to ask the questions that matter most, instead of simply relying on the same old questions that gather the same old information. Skillful questions help evaluate your skills and passions, not just your degrees and years of experience.

3. *Step Out of Your Comfort Zone*
   Neale Donald Walsch says that "life begins at the end of your comfort zone" (quoted in Vinod 2015), and this is especially true in the hiring process. Staying within the rigid methods and mindsets that have ruled the hiring industry for decades will not get you the hires or jobs you want. To make something extraordinary happen, you must take some chances and shift away from comfort and familiarity.

4. *Take Your Time and Do It Right*
   The standard hiring process privileges speed and volume above the patience and skillfulness that lead to long-term retention. When businesses, applicants, and recruiters take their time and do it right, they tend to get the result they want faster and more effectively, with less trial and error.

5. *Be a Hunter*
   In ancient human societies, there were individuals who hunted and those who gathered, and both skills were vital for survival. But in the modern business community, long-term success belongs to those who are willing to take the initiative and seek the right employees, the right jobs, and the right opportunities.

Getting Under the Hood

The Faremouth Method works because it gets under the hood of the resume, looking for vital information about the applicant's passions, experiences, and sense of purpose. We begin by asking the applicant a different set of questions when we interview them. Of course, we start with the traditional questions about education and experience, but then we dig deeper; that's where we find the gold. When you find out who the person really is and get behind their resume, you learn so much more about what lights them up and what makes them tick. If a recruiter is willing to discover what the applicant likes to do, then they can align the applicant with the right job, where they will stick and stay for a long time, becoming an asset to the company. Isn't that what most employers are looking for? Hiring is expensive for employers. When a company hires someone, they are making a huge investment. And it's even more expensive to make a bad hire. It's not good for the applicant either; no one wants to continuously change jobs. It's grueling to interview and take a job, let alone continue to do it again and again.

Going beyond Technology to Find the Perfect Employee

Not long ago, I was concerned my job would be replaced by technology. I have been a recruiter since 1982, but all the new search engines that have been cropping up in recent years had me worried. However, I've come to realize that many of those fears were unfounded. It's become clear that our success as recruiters will be our ability to bring our own unique skills to function alongside vital technology.

There was one company who had listed a job on one of the popular search engines, and it had not been filled for over ninety days. It was a job at a chemical plant for an environmental engineer. The engineering candidate I had was outstanding and fit the job description perfectly. So I picked up the phone and called the company and spoke to the person in charge of hiring for the job. When I mentioned the position had not been filled in over ninety days, he went on to tell me he was paying a huge amount of money to one of the job boards and could not justify paying a recruiter as well. "Okay," I said. "But how much is it going to cost if you have an environmental violation or an accident at your plant because this job is unfilled and you have to pay a steep fine?" He told me it "could cost millions of dollars." He then agreed to let me come over and talk to him about my services. When I went to meet him, I brought the candidate's resume with me, and I explained to him how I did my job. I told him I not only matched experience to a job—which was not a problem for my candidate—but also looked at the whole person and what they could bring to a company. I also told him I needed to understand his company and the features of the available position. He went on to describe the company to me, what made a good employee, and the skill set required for the job. He told me he had never had a recruiter take the time to understand his company, which could never be done by merely viewing a job description on a job board. We went on to discuss the candidate and how his skills aligned well with the job, and he eventually interviewed and hired the candidate. Afterward, I ended up placing several more people with the company, turning it into a multi-hire account. It took me away from the office for several hours that day, but I ended up building a relationship with the company for many years to come.

This is not to say that job boards don't fill a necessary step in the hiring process, but at times, it might not be enough. Understanding people versus identifying them is something to consider. This engineer not only had the skill set the client needed, but he lived close to the company, was looking for career advancement, and had completed an internship (which was not on his resume) with a chemical company that was helpful to him in being successful in this role. He ended up being promoted and is still with the company after many years.

We do live in an age where technology is a necessary part of our lives, but sometimes we must consider that it is only part of the process and may not be enough to get the job done right. There are many articles these days about the human element being eliminated through the rise of technology. But for savvy recruiters, the human element can never be replaced. Can just looking at a resume tell us the entire story about how good of a match we can make? If a company has the personnel available to ask the right questions, look beyond the resume, and align the candidates to the jobs, it might be successful. But oftentimes, a company recruiter is not trained to do this. I've had many conversations with clients who have had heavy turnover. Often, I hear that the resume looked right on paper but the candidate did not stay long, and they are not sure why.

For me, the ability to make solid placements is a form of art. When you are composing a piece of art, you use both facts and intuition to compose your work. The artist is trained in her field and her perseverance, patience, and vision all matter a great deal. We can apply this same method to making a good placement. If we know the right questions to ask both the company and the candidate, we can make the right placement, without years of trial and error. And the same perseverance, patience, and vision matter a great deal in being a successful recruiter. When we get it right, the company gets a longer-tenured employee because the applicant's needs are met. Technology is here to stay. There is no doubt about that. But when we use it to make a successful hire, we should consider it as a step in the process and not the process in and of itself.

Making the Match

As human beings, we make all kinds of matches in our lives. But making the right match in your career is vital. Being aligned to a job that resonates with who you are and utilizes your skills and abilities can bring you tremendous satisfaction that will spill over into other areas of your life.

Lori Greiner is a famous entrepreneur, "The Queen of QVC," and a regular on the program *Shark Tank*, which gives many new entrepreneurs funding to develop and expand their businesses. One of my favorite quotes from Lori is, "I've always believed you hire character and train skill" (quoted in McKale 2016). And as all great recruiters know, there is a great deal of truth to those words.

For many years—and still to this day—recruiters and hiring authorities have relied on a match between a job description and a resume to consider a prospective candidate qualified for an interview. The personal character of the candidate was not a variable to be considered. But after many years of successful recruiting, I know that aligning the correct character to a company is an important ingredient to making a good match. And changing how we select candidates is something we all must begin to do as our global economy changes and we are forced to consider new ways of hiring. For successful recruiters, a great match is a strong connection between an applicant and a business, helping them form a partnership for the benefit of both parties. The hiring authority or recruiter needs to have a clear understanding of both parties' needs and requirements to make a good match. A real match is sustainable and lasts for many years.

Five Features of a Good Match

1. The match serves both parties.

2. Both parties are satisfied and reap rewards and benefits from the match.

3. The match produces high-quality work.

4. The match lasts for many years.

5. The match allows both parties to grow and develop.

Matching Paper vs. Matching People

Can just looking at a resume tell you all you need to know about a candidate? The short answer is no. Resumes and formal interviews have always been the traditional method of hiring. Recruiters and companies usually just match a resume (one piece of paper) to a job description (another piece of paper). But what are we missing here? Shouldn't there be a better way to screen people?

The old practice of simply matching the anonymity of paper instead of matching the humanity of people has been a contributing factor to the current crisis in retention. Resumes show select information about a person's past and history, information that may be vital in understanding the candidate. But a resume cannot show you who that person is today. The only constant in life is change; people are a variable product and they are always changing. There is no resume or assessment tool that can help you understand a person's skills, values, passions, and commitments; we only come to understand those things if we are willing to ask the deeper questions and listen to the answers. This is the heart of The Faremouth Method, and the process results in an invitation to a candidate to do a job that meets the core needs of their personality.

The Faremouth Method is a holistic approach to hiring. In other words, it considers all knowledge in the process of hiring—of the nature, functions, and properties of a whole's components, as well as their interaction with each other and their relationship to the whole. One candidate's personality type might require job stability, while another candidate thrives on change. Maybe the candidate works best in isolation. Maybe they need a high degree of control over their environment or to use their hands to make things. You can't get all that information by simply looking at a resume. It just can't be done.

To prepare a candidate for future growth and development, we must discover what drives them and what career will engage their purpose and passion today.

The Unhirable Princeton Grad

I recently had a company rule out a well-qualified candidate by simply looking at her resume. The candidate had received a degree from Princeton, but her work history looked inconsistent. Her resume showed she had changed jobs several times. What it didn't show was that her husband's career took him to different cities and, when he moved, she moved with him. Her resume showed she worked at one company for six years but then stayed at another company for only eighteen months. What it didn't show was that she left after eighteen months because the company went into bankruptcy and closed its doors. The candidate was now divorced and no longer required to move frequently. She was adaptable to change but was now able to commit fully to a new job. The candidate had completely different life circumstances, which her resume alone could not portray. All her references praised her as a high achiever—a person who had worked for a start-up and who worked long hours to accomplish the tasks assigned to her. Her performance reviews were outstanding, but the company she was interested in could not get past the holes and inconsistencies on her resume, so they declined to interview her.

The ironic part of this story is that the candidate went on to work for one of the company's major competitors. The person who declined to interview her recently mentioned to me how sorry he now is that he didn't hire her. The woman he wasn't even willing to meet was promoted within her first year with the new company and has turned out to be one of their best employees. Maybe if the first company had looked beyond her resume and asked a different set of questions, they would be the ones with the great employee.

The Hardworking Hairdresser

Recently, I went on a trip to the Texas Hill Country for the Fourth of July. My sons, their then fiancés, and I stayed at a resort, and while the boys went fishing, we girls went to a local café for breakfast. My older son's fiancé was facing a woman sitting at a nearby table and couldn't take her eyes off this whopper of a diamond ring the woman was wearing. She mentioned that she loved the ring and apologized for staring at it, which started a conversation between the two women that went on for quite some time. The woman introduced herself as Cathy and invited us over to see the new house she was building in the Hill Country. Later, we decided to go have dinner at a nearby restaurant, where she told us her amazing story.

Cathy was a successful business development representative for a title company, but her only formal training had been as a hairdresser. She had worked at a salon in her hometown for a few years and had had many steady customers. One of her customers happened to be the successful owner of a title company, as well as the owner of a famous sports team. He really liked Cathy and was impressed with her personality, intelligence, and character. He asked her if she might consider working for him a few days a week to learn the title business. She was reluctant to do it, but when he told her how lucrative it could be and how successful he thought she would be, she agreed to give it a try. This man had the keen ability to assess a person's skill set and align those skills to a successful position. Cathy started working for this man part-time and still did hair a couple days a week. The owner saw she was a natural at the job and sent her to formalized training for the industry.

Cathy said that after only two months, she started closing deals left and right. She told us she would come home at night and study all the materials she had been given in the formal training program. She was passionate about this job and enjoyed working with the people in the field. After Cathy became a top producer, she moved up the ladder in the company and became a manager. After only a year, the owner put her in charge of opening other offices all over the country. At the end of four years, she had opened sixty offices and had a staff of over a hundred people under her. The company was applauded as the most successful title company of the major metropolitan city in which it was based. After less than seven years, the company was sold at an enormous profit for the owner, and Cathy went on to take a senior-level position with a competitor. Her service orientation and her ability to understand the customer transferred into another industry. Had this title company owner not been willing to take a risk and shape her raw talent, he might not have landed such a good employee and had the successful business he did. Cathy ended up building three homes and raising two successful children as a single parent. It's interesting to see the wonderful results that can happen when a person can use their skill set and (with the proper training) bloom and prosper.

Strategy Is Better than Luck

Some people think that getting or not getting the right job or the right hire is simply a matter of luck. But we make our own luck. There's a saying credited to many that luck is what happens when preparation meets opportunity. We have to prepare for a different way of screening candidates if we want the opportunity to make better hires. This is a unique time in corporate culture and in the economy; we have different hiring challenges than we have ever had before. Our global society is transforming in many ways as well.

People want more fulfillment at work. They want a job that resonates with their core being—with who they are—and not just what school they went to or what they know how to do.

The Faremouth Method is the first step in a hiring strategy that has a greater chance to match the candidates of today with the quality workplace and life experience they are seeking. These more strategic matches ensure retention, high productivity, and success.

Loving and Hating Your Job

Have you ever had a job you hated? Think about it right now. Think about how little loyalty you felt to your employer when the job didn't meet your needs. Think about how you hated to get up every morning and go into work. When we are looking for a job, we need to do a self-inventory. A lot of candidates coming out of college don't know what they want to do. Many, unfortunately, have not had enough job experiences to really identify what they want to do. Often, people come out of school and discover that the subject they studied and worked hard to get a degree in has nothing to do with who they really are and what they are destined to do in life. As a seasoned recruiter, I've heard all the stories. They go something like this: "Well, my dad was an engineer, and he told me that is what I should do." Or "I liked math and numbers, so I thought being an accountant would be a good field of study for me." Or "I've heard doctors make a lot of money, so I thought I should go to medical school." Then they end up taking a job in those fields, and they are miserable. Why does this happen? Well, sometimes we just don't spend enough time identifying what we are passionate about and what jobs would utilize our skill sets.

There is a common saying often attributed to Confucius: "Choose a job you love, and you will never work a day in your life." This doesn't mean we wouldn't have to work. It simply means the job wouldn't seem like work because it would utilize those passions we have as human beings. It would be helpful if there were courses at the high school level designed to help people identify their passions. But as I'm sure such courses are not a part of most high school curriculums, there might be another way to skin this cat. We are defined by what we do in a job or career, and we need to do some deep soul-searching to find out what our real passions are. If you are the type of person who gets much joy out of helping people, ask yourself what careers are out there that would utilize those skill sets. The truth is that sometimes who a person was in the past or what field of study they have chosen to take does not align with who they are in the present. To be a real human being, and not a "human doing," takes some assessment. Sometimes going back to your hobbies and real interests can lead you to a career you will love. And sometimes we have to take many jobs before we find the right one. But we can save a lot of time in this process if we understand what our passions are and align ourselves to a job that will fulfill those passions and commitments.

Millennials and Boomers: Where Technology Meets Relationships

If you are of the millennial generation and you are being interviewed by a baby boomer for a job (or vice versa!), there are some specific challenges you might face. In a down market especially, both generational groups must learn to communicate a bit differently. No matter what group you belong to, what matters most is getting a good offer and making a good match.

Let's imagine a candidate, John, a senior technical sales engineer with over thirty years' experience in the oilfield service industry. John survived three rounds of layoffs, but because of a major downturn in the market and cost-cutting measures, he was let go. In his last job, John had always had administrative staff to handle all his sales reports, putting them on an Excel spreadsheet for him. He doesn't know anything about contact management systems, which many of his colleagues and competitors use, but John is a real relationship guy and knows how to relate to the people who have the authority to place the orders.

So let's go through the process John might have recently

experienced while being interviewed by a millennial MBA who had an opening for a sales engineer. If John had been coached by a recruiter on doing his homework before the interview and countering any of his interviewer's objections, the interview process might go something like this:

Millennial MBA: Nice to meet you, John. Your tenure is impressive. It's rare these days to see a person with fifteen years in one job. Why do you think you stayed in that job for so long, and what were the accomplishments you were most proud of?

John: Thank you for inviting me in today. I stayed with the company for fifteen years because I enjoyed what I did and was proud to be able to make major contributions that allowed the company to triple its sales during my tenure there. I've cultivated many relationships throughout the years, and I know all I need to do is pick up the phone and my contacts will buy from me, no matter where I land. I have a book of business to bring in the door.

Millennial MBA: So how did you cultivate these relationships through the years? What was your method, and how did you market your product to reach such a wide audience?

John: I joined a lot of professional organizations and did a lot of networking. Since our industry is about relationships, people knew me from my reputation of having a lot of satisfied customers. I also did a lot of cold-calling and played the numbers.

Millennial MBA: Cold-calling is the dinosaur way of marketing these days, John. We use contact management systems and sophisticated technology to cast a wider net and work smarter as opposed to harder. How are you going to get up to speed with today's technology?

John: I've already done my homework in that regard. I've taken tutorials online already to bring me up to speed with technological advances. That's the easy part. You can know all the technology in the world, but if your prospective customers don't trust your reputation or your knowledge of their products and services, all the technology in the world won't get them to buy from you.

Millennial MBA: How do I know you will be able to relate to other millennial MBAs like myself? There is a big difference in work ethic and attitude. How are you going to be able to get them to want to work with you?

John: I've done my homework on that front as well. I know there are many generational differences between millennials and baby boomers. But at the end of the day, we can both benefit and succeed from a blending of the two styles. You millennial MBAs can assist us with perfecting our technological skills, while we baby boomers can teach you how to put down your smartphones and relate to other human beings. A blending of the two styles can be mutually beneficial. I also know that neither style is better or worse; they're just different. Both methods are necessary to get the job done in our current market. And so long as we both know we have differences going in, it makes the end result a lot more worthwhile and less stressful.

Millennial MBA: This all sounds great, John. But what are your actual references going to say about you? How do I know all this is not just fabricated but that it is in fact true?

John: I had a feeling you might ask for references, so here is a list of six of my recent bosses and supervisors who have given me permission to have you call them. I encourage you to give them a call.

Millennial MBA: Also, John, your salary of $159K is a bit steep for this market. How flexible are you willing to be?

John: I will be flexible considering the current market. I know I have much to contribute, but I will certainly consider a fair offer.

Millennial MBA: We have several more interviews to conduct before we bring back the final five contenders. Thanks for coming in, and we will get back with you.

John: Thank you for having me come in. By the way, I did some research on the big projects your company may be bidding on. Let me show you a list of those projects and the people I know who would allow us to get in the door quickly and onto their vendor list.

Millennial MBA: Wow, John. You did do your homework, and I must say, I'm impressed. I'll let my VP know about this and we will definitely be getting back with you.

So as you can see, John did do his homework. And he showed the millennial MBA areas where technology would not be the main advantage. Knowing people who would have the power to put this company on the spec list meant dollars in the door to this interviewer. Technology without relationships is only half of the equation. But John had to be proactive before the interview and do his homework to be able to compete in today's market.

Passion Drives People

Staying true to our passions as human beings can lead us to our true destiny. Our passions inspire and motivate us; they drive us forward and remind us of what we truly care about. Whether you are an applicant looking for the perfect job, an employer looking for the perfect employee, or a recruiter stumped to make a solid placement, the following steps can assist you on your own journey. A successful job search is like finding a kind of home—a special place where we belong.

For the Applicant

You have to be in touch with your own special gifts and talents to recognize the perfect job that could be your home. Know what makes your heart sing, and you will be well on your way to finding the answer to your quest. When you align yourself with your passions and desires in the workplace, you will find meaningful employment that will give you the motivation to perform well and achieve much. Be authentic. Do what makes you happy. Don't follow the path others think is your special destiny. A thorough self-inventory is necessary to arrive at this special place. If you are unsure of what your gifts and talents are, perhaps taking an assessment test can assist you in finding the perfect job or career.

For the Employer

Understanding your company's culture is crucial to determining what type of person will fit with your corporate goals and values. Clearly identify the positions in your company and make a list of objectives you need the employee to achieve. Having a vague job description or lacking specific achievement milestones can make it difficult to secure the best candidate for your position. I see it all the time when a client calls me with a loose job description. Or they send me a job description so out of line with the corporate goals, they end up hiring a person who is a totally wrong fit. Making a bad hire is a costly mistake and ultimately affects the bottom line. Don't get hung up on finding resumes that read well. If an employee has the passion, desire, and proven track record of success and will fit in with your company's culture, they can be trained to be a stellar performer. Sometimes, thinking outside the box is the key here. A recent client named me a "talent agent" because my real job is to identify a candidate's talents and align them to a job that will engage those talents. Statistics have demonstrated that high IQ and experience might not be the most important credentials to secure in a candidate. The risk in making a bad hire is much lower when emotional intelligence and passion for the job are paired together.

For the Recruiter

I hear my professional affiliates complain about not being able to find experienced candidates. Well, they are looking in the wrong place. They are looking for experienced people with resumes that read the way their clients are telling them they need to read. They need to get on board, and quickly, to the fact that such people are not usually available and the shortage of talent is only going to get worse. Successful recruiters begin by considering alternative methods of hiring and educating their clients on the benefits and advantages of hiring a new breed of employees. It has to start with the recruiters getting on board. If they don't, they might have to choose a different career path. It's harder and harder to make a living as a recruiter these days, but it doesn't have to be. We just need to operate in a different manner and offer our clients passionate, proven, intelligent employees. Such applicants are out there; we just have to use a different net to catch these new fish. The old road is not going to get us where we need to go.

CHAPTER 2
BUSINESS AS USUAL

How We Got Here

The history of the American worker is a long and complicated one. To get to where we are today, the US workforce has experienced decades of reform, change, revolution, and innovation. From the days when products were brought to market by the horse and buggy, to the evolution of high technology and robotics, this transformation has taken years to achieve. And the defeat of many discriminatory business laws and practices have been critically important achievements as well. These days, we sit in our air-conditioned offices and take for granted our hour for lunch and our ability to receive time and a half for overtime; we often forget that these are all still relatively modern inventions.

And yet here we are, not long after the stock market crashed in 2008 and oil prices plummeted 50 percent in 2014, still rebuilding the economy and our broken job market. In *The Talent Equation*, the authors state that:

> between 2000 and the end of the 2007 recession, the U.S. lost approximately 5.5 million manufacturing jobs. The culprits [were] largely the forces of globalization and automation. But to the surprise of many economists, a positive trend started in late 2011 and early 2012: Manufacturing went through its first period of sustained job growth since the 1990s. The sector has added 265,000 jobs post-recession. And although it barely made a dent compared to the loss column, economists saw this as welcome news. After a half century of offshoring factory labor, the cost curve is bending back in the favor of the U.S. Moreover, technological innovation such as 3D

printing of product prototypes allows small firms to go to market more quickly, which increases the incentive to stay in North America. James Fallows of *The Atlantic* magazine wrote that such developments could foretell a "renaissance" of manufacturing startups in the U.S. (Ferguson, Hitt, and Tambe 2013, 295)

Surges and Slumps

In every branch of the business world, the only constant is change. In my home industry, oil and gas, the boom in oil prices is often followed by a slump. As of today, almost three hundred thousand people have been let go in Houston, Texas, alone. Oil has dropped, and it seems those in the oil-related industries have been on a dangerous roller coaster ride since December 2014. And more cuts seem to be coming. But oil and gas is only one segment of the market. And although this is certainly a reason to be concerned about this industry, the employment world has other problems to consider—like those related to the looming skills gap we face.

Even if your firm has a healthy employee base and a strong balance sheet, chances are good that it's about to face a significant shortage of qualified managers.

In 2014, Claudio Fernández-Aráoz (2014) worked with the dean of Harvard Business School and colleagues at the executive search firm Egon Zehnder to gauge the effects of three factors—globalization, demographics, and leadership pipelines—on competition for senior talent in large organizations. They studied forty-seven companies, spanning all major sectors and geographies. The results were dire: only 15 percent of the firms in the Americas and Asia, and less than a third of those in Europe, had enough people primed to lead them into the future. Survey and research data compiled more recently show that the situation has grown even worse.

This situation can be traced to a time after World War II. After the war, when all the soldiers returned home, there was a surge in the population. The babies born then are what we now refer to as baby boomers, and many of those folks will be looking to retire soon.

Many firms do not have the proper people in the pipeline to replace these senior employees. A decade ago, the shortage of rising leaders affected mostly the United States and Europe; however, experts say that by 2020 many other large economies, including Russia, Canada, South Korea, and China, will have more people at retirement age than entering the workforce. And reports by many have stated that companies are not properly developing their pipelines of future leaders. Unfortunately, this is not new information; in a 2014 PwC survey of CEOs in sixty-eight countries, 63 percent were concerned about the future availability of key skills at all levels (PwC 2014).

This is going to create a pressing demand for the right talent in the right places over the coming decade, which will lead to a war for talent and unprecedented challenges for most organizations. But it also presents a huge opportunity for leaders who are determined to surround themselves with the best people and to equip their organizations with the right hiring, retention, and development strategies (ensuring a strong focus on potential).

So now is the time to identify what your company culture is all about and gather people to it that reflect your own set of values. Now is your time to build up, not break down. It's time to find your perfect matches. Even if you have short-tenured, more inexperienced people, you can train them or align them with more experienced folks who have cultivated the business relationships that can bring in fast sales and affect the bottom line quickly.

Alternative methods of hiring, like The Faremouth Method, must be implemented now to prepare our organizations for the serious problem looming right around the corner. Solutions are available, but we need to act now to prepare for this situation before it's too late.

The Skills Gap

After many years of placing people in the manufacturing sector, I can see the renaissance of jobs that James Fallows predicted. America currently has millions of job openings available—more than at any point since the year 2000. And for the economy, you might think this is all good news. But from my side of the desk—

dealing with the challenge of finding qualified people to fill these jobs—several factors prevent this resurgence from living up to its potential:

- Experts say that job training programs in the United States remain lackluster compared to the country's global peers in Europe and Asia.

- The jobs this nation has created in the last two years differ greatly from the ones lost following the 2008 financial crisis.

- Our intuition about the world of work needs to be reset. An approximate average of thirty people apply to a single job opening, yet according to the Corporate Executive Board, only about 35 percent of those applicants meet the qualifications for the job (K@W 2012).

All of these point to a single major problem: the emerging skills gap. The demand for qualified candidates is overwhelming the supply. In the manufacturing sector alone, "rapidly deployed new technologies, major demographic shifts, and corporate globalization have employers scouring for qualified candidates. It's estimated that as many as 600,000 manufacturing positions are currently unfilled in the U.S." (Kaslow 2012, 36). And this trend can be seen throughout various other sectors as well, including technology and healthcare.

To correct this trend, training programs must be strongly implemented to enhance employee and employer productivity. There is no one true method available to secure the perfect employee or employer. All parties must be mindful of the challenging market conditions and work together to find solutions.

And solutions are available, *if* we can change the mindset of three groups: candidates, recruiters, and company employers. The only way our workforce and global economy will continue to grow and prosper is if these groups quickly come to understand the growing problem, through facts and statistics, and identify and implement potential solutions.

As for the manufacturing sector, to ensure that such companies can continue bringing a variety of products to the marketplace, we need the *right* people to do these jobs. Having jobs open for months on end only slows production and causes a severe lack of productivity. The loss of productivity translates into a loss of profits, which in turn leads to a weaker economy. It's time to stop complaining about the problem and start taking serious steps to solve it. The American workforce has had a long history of revolution. This book is part of the next one. The Faremouth Method will guide you through five important steps that can lead to solutions for the three groups mentioned above, allowing them to get the wheels of productivity turning once more. If we work together to bring about awareness and cooperation, all parties can realize positive solutions to our employment needs.

Whether the Market Is Up or Down, the Steps of The Faremouth Method Remain the Same.

When I began writing this book in January 2014, the city and market I was serving was in a glorious up cycle. Oil was at an all-time high—over a hundred dollars per barrel—and our industry was rocking and rolling. New manufacturing plants, as well as distribution companies, were popping up all over the country. Clients were calling me in deep distress because they had orders to process, sales to make, profits to be accounted for, and no people to fill the positions. There was a serious lack of employees capable of handling the strong demands, and The Faremouth Method was an alternative method of hiring I had been using for many years. And it worked. It got under the hood of the resume and tapped into the whole person, not just their skills, educational background, etc. We placed many people who, on paper, looked completely wrong for the job, yet most of those people are still performing in the same jobs—many in upwardly mobile positions.

Now, three years later, the market has shifted, sliding into a deep trough. Oil is down, and large corporations in the industry I serve are downsizing and changing their business models to survive this recent crisis. Yet The Faremouth Method is just as flexible and valuable a tool as it always has been. When businesses need to make a strategic hire, it's more important than ever to ask the right questions, clearly assess the position you are offering, and step out of your comfort zone to find the right people. When many candidates are competing for a limited number of positions, it's vital they dig deep for the full range of their passions, interests, and skills and be a hunter—not simply relying on their employment history or academic degrees, hoping the right job will magically come their way.

No matter where the market stands, the steps of The Faremouth Method can help you make the right match at the right time.

The Old Model

The old model recruiters and businesses have always used is matching one piece of paper to another—a job description to a resume. It's posting a job on a job board, reviewing resumes, interviewing, and then hiring. But this method isn't working.

I had a client call me recently, extremely frustrated. She had done all those things, interviewed thirty-two people, and still had not filled the job. She went on to describe the job to me and told me it was not a difficult job to fill. She said she had used countless recruiters and posted the position on several job boards, but after two months, the job remained unfilled. When I asked her what the crucial elements of the jobs were, she told me she needed a degree, ten years of experience, bilingual Spanish, advanced Excel skills, field experience in the pipeline equipment business, and a willingness to travel. I understood then why she hadn't filled the job. I explained to her that many of her must-haves might be incompatible with one another. An excellent field person with such a level of experience might not have the technical skills on her list. When I suggested I come out to the company and talk with the hiring manager, she said she didn't have time. She had a deadline to fill this job: the end of the week. I explained that if we did it the way she suggested we would be going in circles, and that is not how I do my job. I needed to get more information about the critical aspects of the job and meet the people in the department; only then would I be able to fill the position promptly. When she told me she didn't want to do it that way, I recommended she call another recruiter.

Eventually, she agreed to have me meet the department head, and I went out to the company the next day. When that hiring authority began to tell me how frustrated he was because this was such an "easy job to fill," I told him that, on the contrary, the job was not fillable at all. He looked at me like I had come from another planet. I went on to explain that we essentially had two options. One was to raise the salary by about $20K in order to attract a person with ten years of experience. The other was to loosen or drop some of the requirements and bring in a more junior person who could then be trained. He argued that he needed a person totally fluent in Spanish as they would be dealing with Mexico and South America daily. They had to have strong knowledge of equipment, such as casing, tubing pipe, valves, and fittings, and their application in the field. He also claimed to need an Excel expert who could type up sophisticated reports for the company's vice president.

I told him I could find him a bilingual applicant fluent in Spanish who understood equipment specifications, but if they didn't have the computer-based skills he required then the company could either send them to advanced Excel training or have another employee type up the reports. He agreed to drop the advanced Excel skills but then tried to lower the salary. I told him that would not work. Such a position was in high demand at the time, and the applicants he sought were in short supply and at premium salaries.

Then I asked him a couple of important questions: How much was it costing him in production to not have a person in this position? And how much overtime was he himself putting in to get the job done?

His answer was that he was working twelve- to fourteen-hour days, losing business to the competition, and upsetting his remaining customers. I told him that there was his answer. It would be much less expensive to pay a bit more for the right person than to continue this merry-go-round of interviews for a person who was not available at the salary he wanted to pay. So we raised the salary offer, and he interviewed three more people. He had a hard time deciding which one to hire, but in the end, he made a great match.

This placement only happened because I didn't just match a resume to a set of job specifications. I took the time to understand the client's needs, as well as identify candidates who would align with the job.

Business as usual is anything but usual these days. We need to change the mindset of companies to be realistic for the times we are dealing with. We need to look at the whole person and what transferrable skills they may have. How the resume reads doesn't solve the problem. We need to understand both sides of the fence here to make a good hiring decision. We are in different times. When economies shift and we go through severe changes in the marketplace, we must also change our methods of hiring. That is what this book is all about.

The PowerPoint Pipe Salesman

I had a client who wanted to hire a salesperson to sell software to the pipe industry. The software was a pipe traceability product that ensured the pipe was properly identified and labeled correctly. They were very firm about wanting a person with a software background, a degree in IT, and an ability to explain the technicalities of the software. I listened carefully to what the client was telling me they wanted, and I knew right away this type of profile probably wouldn't work in the industry. As I've been working with the pipeline service industry for over thirty years, I know the culture well. A technical person without the relationship skills to relate to these people probably would not be successful. The product was marketed to oilfield people, but someone walking into their office and only talking about software applications would be like someone attempting a conversation with them in a foreign language. They would not understand their method of communication. Even so, I listened to the client and suggested we see a variety of people. I told them their product was somewhat unique, but I thought we should discuss our options.

I started sending them resumes for their review. The resumes they initially reviewed were people with technical backgrounds and sales experience. They interviewed them and told me they wanted to see more. I interviewed a candidate who had worked in the industry in an inventory / sales support role and was degreed in business with a strong technical aptitude. She had a burning desire to do outside sales but was not able to progress to such a role with her current company. Her previous job had entailed inventorying pipe, including damaged or surplus pipe, which would have become easier with the availability of the traceability product. When I told her about the open position, she immediately became excited. She told me she wanted to go on the interview because she knew the need for the product as someone on the other side who saw the results of not using such software.

The client was reluctant to see her, but after my spiel on why she might be a good fit, they agreed to interview her. She had also been interviewing on her own before she came to me and had recently received a whopper of an offer. Almost $20K more than her current salary. I told the client we needed to move fast. After her second interview, they told me the president wanted to see her before they made the final decision since they were still on the fence over her lack of strong outside sales experience. The applicant decided, on her own, to put together a PowerPoint presentation about the advantages of the product. She also illustrated, in her presentation, contacts she had already established who would be interested in buying this product. They flew her up to the main office to meet the president, who was very impressed with her presentation. The candidate had passion about the job but had also established relationships she could bring with her immediately. This meant faster investment return for the client, which would lead to more instant results than any person with a strong technical aptitude but no industry contacts. They hired her, and both parties are extremely happy.

This new method works. The old method of hiring is broken, and I hear about it every single day. It doesn't work because we have a changing economy, a changing employment market, and a supply and demand problem when it comes to applicants. We don't have a choice. We need to consider alternative methods of hiring. Our new employment market is here to stay, and if we don't get on the bandwagon and change how we hire, our bottom line and the way we do business will be directly affected.

The Short Game: How Recruiters Work

Being a recruiter these days isn't easy. And it's only going to get harder. With the current shortage of available talent, recruiters are facing major challenges. According to an article in the November 2014 special supplement of *HR Magazine*, the Bureau of Labor Statistics had predicted that "by 2016 one-third of the U.S. labor force [would] be 50 or older" (Jackson 2014). And a *Gray Tsunami* is indeed upon us. The global aging challenge and shortage of qualified people in the workplace is, without a doubt, a reality. Recruiters have to get on board with these real challenges, and it's important that you find one with the skill set to assist you with your needs.

Working as an executive recruiter for the last thirty years, I've seen my share of recruiters—the good, the not-so-good, and the great. I've worked with and for a wide variety of these people and seen many different styles. The ones with integrity have always won my respect and admiration. In your pursuit of solving your hiring issues, I suggest you interview a prospective recruiter in much the same way you interview a prospective candidate. You must ask important questions on the front-end that will result in a successful experience and will make your choice a positive one.

Most recruiters are called *contingent recruiters*, which essentially means their fee is contingent on them filling a position. This leads to a sense of urgency on their part and a strong desire to fill a job *fast*. After all, the faster they fill a job, the faster they get paid. If a job search—with all the steps involved—is conducted quickly, the end result is usually low retention. Low retention does not serve anyone well. It's a bad investment for the client, the applicant is back to the drawing board again, and the recruiter's reputation is tarnished by the threat of losing the client. Everyone loses. Some recruiters might beg to differ over the benefit of high retention; as far as they are concerned, if an applicant stays long enough to at least uphold the placement guarantee and then leaves, oftentimes their recruiter can then place them in another job and collect another fee. I am solidly against this practice. When I make a solid placement and the person stays for a long time, that's when I really end up making more fees. A client who is happy with an employee and their work product will oftentimes send me their clients, vendors, and even family members. At the same time, the happy employee sends me their friends, and trusting associate recruiters send me their jobs. The one fee I might have made with a short-tenured employee would not have resulted in the volume placements and volume fees I have made with the trust I've earned with all three involved parties.

Another concerning fact about the way many recruiters work is that they resist looking under the hood of the resume. They are so stuck in the traditional methods of hiring—of matching the paper of a resume to the paper of a job order—that they totally miss the human element. Essentially, they don't take the time to do it right. They don't ask the right questions. They don't take into consideration current market conditions, and their primary intent is to rush the process and make a fee.

How to Get It Wrong

Let me tell you a story of a recent experience I had with a referring recruiter's candidate. Let's call the recruiter Sandy. Sandy sent me the resume of a candidate we will call Jill for an inside sales position. Jill's last three jobs had been inside sales within my client's industry. When I reviewed the resume, I noticed that the last three jobs had also been short-tenured jobs. When I brought Jill in to interview for my current opening, I learned many disconcerting facts about her. Jill told me she had been laid off from her last three jobs. As I reviewed the dates of her tenure, I found that hard to believe as they were all during boom times of the market when clients rarely did layoffs. After asking her a series of questions, I learned that she hadn't actually been laid off; she had been *fired.* When I dug deeper and asked more questions, I also found out that Jill didn't even want to do inside sales; she preferred to keep her head down and did not enjoy working with people or countering objections. Finally, she told me her real passion and joy was working with computers, generating reports, and working with the inventory aspects of the job. I then asked her if her last few jobs were short-tenured because she had not been in alignment with what she wanted to do. She really opened up to me then. When I suggested we might look at an inventory job, where her main tasks were more focused on assembling data, she agreed. Had the referring recruiter taken the time to understand their applicant, a lot of valuable time would not have been wasted. When I contacted Sandy, the referring recruiter, and explained my findings to her, she responded by saying, "Well, her resume looked like a perfect match." I politely told her that looking only at the resume is a dangerous endeavor. She made many excuses, and I eventually hung up the phone.

The Faremouth Method is a system of placement that puts the client and applicant first and the recruiter last. But all parties benefit from this method, and recruiters generally become more successful by shifting their focus from the fee to taking the time to make a good match.

Time for a Change

What do we mean when we talk about change? Our lives start changing from the moment we are born. The change happens on a cellular level, and we know the only constant in life is change. Any organism that doesn't change, dies, since change is a natural part of life. Any person that doesn't learn new skills, stops growing. So why would changing the way we hire be so different? As a recruiter, when clients tell me they have had huge turnover in a position or the people they have hired have not been star performers, could we possibly need to change the way we hire to get a better alignment between employee and employer?

Five Reasons Change Is Necessary in Our Hiring Methods:

1. We are experiencing a skills gap where experienced workers may not be available.

2. A resume doesn't reflect who the person is now, only a summary of what they have accomplished to date.

3. A resume only reflects skills and not the attitude or personality of the applicant.

4. Only matching a resume to a position doesn't show the total package of the person and doesn't evaluate the alignment between employer and employee.

5. Matching one piece of paper to another removes the human element, which is an important part of making a good match.

Resistance to Change

In my recruiting practice, I work in an industry that has been very resistant to change. Corporate hiring managers, recruiting professionals, and company presidents in many cases still choose to rely only on how the resume reads. We are averse to change. After all, we've been doing it this way for so long that many don't know of any other way. But over the years, people have been startled by the results of using this new method. And these days, I get so many referrals from satisfied customers that I think this new method is starting to catch on.

Getting beyond the resume is the only way we can make sure we are hiring the right person for the job. Using The Faremouth Method will require extra time in the interview process, but this investment will pay off in the future. When employees are placed in jobs based on a deeper and more meaningful set of factors, they will stay on the job longer and be more productive, because they are in jobs they really like. And the employers will have employees who want to come to work because the jobs are aligned with their passions. I say it's a win for all involved. You can teach someone how to do a job, but you can't teach passion and commitment. If that's not there, it doesn't matter how much experience they have; they will end up leaving, and you will be right back to looking for another employee. Employers and recruiters alike can be taught to utilize this new model. It's effective, saves time in the long run, and produces astounding results.

A global client I have worked with for over ten years—with whom I have placed salespeople, as well as accounting and administrative staff—called me recently with a critical job to fill. My contact told me she was looking for a systems administrator. The company wanted a local candidate, since they did not want to pay relocation costs. Now, the recent job market here in Houston has been challenging, and the company happened to be involved in the pipeline service area, which has been hit hard because of the downturn in oil prices.

Originally, the company had given the job to a recruiting firm that specialized in IT placement, but the job had remained open for two months with no suitable candidates identified. When the HR manager called me, she was at her wits' end. I suggested widening the net and looking outside of the local market to see if we could have more success. I further explained that if the job had been open for two months, the production they were losing could possibly cost them more than relocation costs. She agreed to go this route, and I began my search.

I found an extremely qualified candidate in the northeast part of the United States and interviewed him over the phone. When I did my screening, I found he had worked remotely for many well-known clients over the last two years, including a global consumer services company. When I checked his references with this company, the feedback I received was glowing. After much discussion with my client, who had always had in-house employees and was resistant to working with someone remotely, the company agreed to interview him over the phone. After conducting research on similar jobs and presenting my findings to the client, I convinced them that the IT market was changing and that such jobs could be well handled by a remote employee. And when they heard that a company like the global consumer services company operated in such a way, they felt better about giving this new way of hiring a chance. The applicant impressed them during the interview, and after much negotiation, they offered him the job, making a great match for both parties.

This alternative method of hiring is a practice that will become more and more common in the years to come. The demand for experienced people in most careers is overwhelming the supply. There is a shortage of qualified talent in many industries, not only in the pipeline industry where I work. But to get employers, recruiters, and candidates to begin using this new model, we must be willing to accept that the modern realities of hiring and finding a job have changed. If the traditional methods of hiring are not working and not meeting the current needs, then it's time to try something new.

In a rapidly changing economic environment, businesses must continually assess the nature of the work to be done and how this translates into skill sets needed within the workforce. To effectively utilize its human capital, an organization also needs to understand the nature of its workforce. Altering business practices to respond to environmental economic changes is imperative.

How the Market Downturn Can Be Viewed as a Good Thing

Downturns can be viewed as a good thing. Throughout my life, I have learned more from the down times and major challenges than from my successes. If your business has had a severe change or loss of some kind and profits are way down, morale is low, and hope for future recovery is not high, then take the time to do a total reassessment of your company, goals, desires, and plans. There is always a silver lining in any cloud. Downturns can force us to evaluate what is important—things we may have neglected to see when things were on the upswing.

What goes up must come down. Take the downturns as your time to reevaluate what really matters to you and your company and where you want your future to go. The knowledge you gain from these tough times can be invaluable in helping you build a more solid future.

CHAPTER 3

THE FAREMOUTH METHOD

Finding a New Model: Matching People to People

The Faremouth Method was born based on overwhelming need. Over a period of a few years, I noticed that most of my established clients all seemed to have the same problem: jobs were going unfilled for months at a time, greatly affecting productivity and hurting their bottom line. There were applicants available, but they lacked the specific experience that the traditional methods of interviewing required us to obtain.

As a recruiting consultant working in Houston, Texas, one of the top cities in the country for jobs since 1982, I sat back in 2012 and tried to analyze the problem. At that time, we had more jobs than any other city in the country, and people were moving here in droves, but we couldn't find the talent we needed to fill the jobs. Salaries were out of sight, and my clients were complaining that they didn't want to pay these unbelievably high salaries. So I began to think about the applicants I currently had available and how I could make them fit the jobs I currently had open.

As a skilled recruiter with a true dedication to solving my client's hiring problems, I began to seek an alternative method that, when utilized, would yield solid results. As I developed this method and began to implement it, the success stories were impressive.

As a person raised in a blue-collar family, nothing ever came easy for me. I had to be resourceful; I had to use my creative skills and available resources to solve life's many challenges. In doing my own soul-searching, I realized that my purpose in life was not my career; rather, my career was guided by my purpose. My real purpose was to make solid placements that would benefit all parties involved. Those parties were my client companies and my applicants. I had always been guided by integrity, a solid work ethic, and honesty. Making solid placements that stuck had always been my main goal. And high retention rates had always been my claim to fame.

What The Faremouth Method requires is looking at the whole person—not just their resume. It considers available skills and their transferability. It looks at implementing on-the-job training programs that would allow intelligent applicants with proven track records to be successful in their jobs. After all, pieces of paper don't show up for work, do they? No, people do. If the correct passion, purpose, dedication, and desire are there for the job, then the person can be trained to do it. And this method does not only apply to those entering the workforce for the first time; as we face the emerging challenge of baby boomers retiring, we must consider strategies and changes in the workforce norm to allow those folks to continue making a valuable contribution.

I've utilized this system of transferring skills into related jobs and industries, and I've had many success stories. This method works; we simply have to change the mindset of our client companies about how they do their hiring. If they ask the right questions in the interview, they will glean important information that will allow them to fill their many open jobs.

The New Model: From *Me* to *We*

This is an era of major upheaval. The pace of change, globally, has never been more rapid. It is unsettling to some and exciting to others. Either way, it's not something we can continue to avoid.

Life and business can't be separated anymore; maybe they never could. Everywhere we look, there is some new article about these revolutionary changes that are penetrating our society. Some call it *Generation Flux*, others the *New Mindset* or the *New Mission*. Whatever you choose to call it, one thing seems perfectly clear: If we don't get on board with these revolutionary changes on our doorstep, we are in trouble. Big trouble. Trouble that translates into heavy turnover, low retention, higher healthcare costs, and for business and corporations in general, loss of revenue and lower profits.

We need new innovative strategic techniques that align an employee's mission to the corporate mission. It's all about matching people to people, not matching people to jobs.

And there are some well-known companies, like Apple, Deloitte, Pepsi, and Eileen Fisher, that have gotten on board with these concepts. They look at the whole person and how that person's unique contributions align with the job they need them to do, which ultimately affects the bottom line.

On the other side of this coin, there are companies like Arthur Andersen. The cultural slide at Arthur Andersen descended through level after level of self-destruction until its ultimate destruction as a company. Arthur Andersen had shifted its focus away from quality, integrity, and moral fiber and moved only toward beating other firms' revenue numbers, which led to its ultimate demise. It was all about the bottom line; the people were not the focus. Profit-seeking tendencies drove the company right into the ground.

Everywhere we go now, we see universal themes of looking at purpose first rather than profits. This distinctive approach has fueled the growth of several companies. Deloitte did a millennial survey in 2016, which showed that millennials want business to shift its purpose (Deloitte 2016, 13).

It seems like we are moving from a *Me* generation to a *We* generation in global business practices. Or could it be that the way we do business is shifting from an *outside-in* approach, where profits are more important than purpose, to an *inside-out* approach, where we look at the whole person and their contributions? It has been said that, the more companies like Apple focus on something beyond money, the more money they make.

These new business leaders represent a rising trend of executives driven not just by money but by the pursuit of a larger societal purpose. Their morality and strong integrity is rewarded in the marketplace. And there is nothing touchy-feely about this new method. Leaders of these high-profit companies are discovering that when they identify a person's passion and channel it into the correct job, people have more meaningful careers. Gallup even reports that "companies with engaged workforces have higher earnings per share" (Sorenson 2013).

Our American workers are human beings, not human doings. When we identify who they are as whole people—not just as cogs in the machine—and align them with a corporate culture that fits who they are, the results are extraordinary.

This alternative method of hiring is a practice we have no choice but to implement. With a majority of baby boomers retiring and an impending shortage of talent, we need a solution. And we need it fast. We can either get on board with this new method, deal with the change in doing business, and reap the huge rewards, or be left in the dust with an old method that no longer serves who we are or how we do business. The choice is ours. But when we evaluate the results of profitable companies using this new method, we realize that this isn't just some pipe dream or new fad for the era. It's a method that aligns beautifully with the twenty-first century and encompasses our larger, more universal global issues.

Emily Esfahani Smith and Jennifer Aaker (2016) have taken this idea even further. They challenged the notion that a pursuit of happiness is what drives us most. Their work suggests that people's satisfaction with life is higher, and of greater duration, when meaning—rather than happiness—is their primary motivation. For other professors, such as Wharton's Adam Grant (2014), this is the difference between a life focused on giving and one focused on taking, a difference he believes increases productivity as well as satisfaction.

We should, of course, stop for a moment to acknowledge that choosing a career built around meaning is not a choice available to billions of people who are desperately struggling just to make enough money to find shelter and put food on the table. That is often the only mission that matters. But for those who have been fortunate enough to look beyond their basic needs, the motivation to do more, create more, and, yes, give more to the world arises directly from the personal meaning we derive from those activities. It's the way humans operate. We are not drones whose only goal is to make more money. Keeping passion out of the workplace makes no sense at all.

Lessons from the Steps of The Faremouth Method

Step 1: Do a Self-Inventory

On a recent trip to San Antonio, I was walking along the River Walk when I ran into a man dressed up like The Tin Man from *The Wizard of Oz*. There was a film festival that weekend, so it wasn't exactly unusual to see people dressed up as film characters. However, I believe I ran into that particular character for a reason. Meeting him reminded me of the story of *The Wizard of Oz* and how The Tin Man's desire for a heart notably contrasted with The Scarecrow's desire for brains. This reflects a common debate between the relative importance of intelligence and emotions. We are all born with gifts, but often we hide them (or have them hidden from us) as children and spend much of our adult years seeking, uncovering, and rediscovering them. Self-discovery is the art of learning to look within ourselves for the answers, but sometimes self-evaluation and self-inventory can be a difficult process.

We all, at times, have felt we weren't good enough. We didn't have the "right stuff" to achieve our goals. We weren't smart enough, weren't emotionally mature enough, or were lacking *something* within ourselves. But The Tin Man, who didn't think he had a heart, turned out to be the most tender and emotional of all Dorothy's companions. Similarly, The Scarecrow, who didn't think he had a brain, was the wisest, and The Cowardly Lion was the bravest. Sometimes, the very qualities we desire but think we lack are right there inside of us, just waiting for us to tap into them.

Step 2: Ask Better Questions

As Dorothy said in *The Wizard of Oz*, there is "no place like home." For many of us, there is nothing like coming home to who we are at the current point in our life. One time, when I was speaking with a technical engineer who had been caught in a layoff situation, I ended up asking a totally different type of question than I normally do. His entire world had been turned upside down. Not only had he lost his job, but his dad had lost a long battle with cancer. The engineer felt horrible that he hadn't been able to spend time with his dad during his final moments because of the strong demands of his job. Also, he had just been informed that his mom had been diagnosed with a different type of cancer, and with his dad gone, he would be required to help her more than ever.

But he kept telling me he needed the same $150K-type salary in his next job. The question I asked him then was this: "What do you *not* want to do in your next job?" He told me he did not want to manage, work long hours, or travel, and he needed a low-stress job. I told him then that I understood his current needs, but those requirements would not translate into a high-paying job, like the management position he had had before. I told him there was something we called "quality of life benefits," which didn't come with a price tag. Although they held no monetary value, the non-material benefits were sometimes worth more than the big dollars.

I placed him in a wonderful job that utilized his skills and allowed him to take care of his personal obligations. He did take a cut in salary, but he tells me he is very happy with the company, has had some raises, and has been able to help his mom with her treatment plan.

Step 3: Step Out of Your Comfort Zone

So how do we tap into these gifts inside of ourselves? How do we allow them to manifest? I think risk is an important exercise. And failure can almost be better than success for some of us; we often learn more about ourselves from failures than we do from success. Trying something we are not totally comfortable with gets us out of our comfort zone and allows us to grow as human beings. It's so much safer and easier to just stay where we are. Staying in a job that you know like the back of your hand and that doesn't allow you to risk failure may seem like the better thing to do. But this choice can be dangerous to our growth and prevents us from getting in touch with gifts and talents we have left lying dormant inside of us. Sometimes we need a tornado, like the one that carried Dorothy to Oz, to shake us up and force us to go to a place we've never been. Losing a job might be your tornado. You may have felt abandoned, angry, rejected, and confused, unable to get back to the feeling of home, where you felt known, valued, and supported.

We work our whole life to self-actualize, but only striving for it and experiencing life allow us to get there. Staying stuck in a safe, easy job doesn't advance anyone. If you are trying to make an important change in your life, look back on your successes and failures and think about the lessons you learned. Stop beating yourself up for what you did wrong, the job that didn't work out, or the mistakes you've made. How many of the successful inventors and entrepreneurs never made a mistake? If you read any successful person's autobiography, you will often find that their failures far surpassed any successes they may have had.

Don't be afraid to risk. Don't be afraid to try. You are an amazing creation, and you have so much inside of you that wants to get out. If you are feeling stuck, you owe it to yourself to go on a new journey. What you find along the way might surprise you.

Step 4: Take Your Time and Do It Right

Sometimes the reward doesn't come right away. I had a client from Europe who was building a plant in Houston. It was critical for him to hire a VP of sales with major contacts and experience in his industry. I had worked almost three months on this placement, weeding through many resumes and interviews until I produced two candidates as finalists. But at the final hour, the client informed me that he was going to bring someone over from the home office instead. I had worked hard on this placement, yet I wasn't going to be allowed to fill it and reap the rewards. I could have given up then, disappointed, and simply moved on to the next job. But I didn't; I kept in touch with the client, and he was so impressed by my strong perseverance and persistence that he insisted on introducing me to

THE FAREMOUTH METHOD

the new VP when he arrived in town. I went to meet the new contact and have since filled many jobs for the company. By taking my time to do it right, even after the rewards appeared to be nonexistent, I managed to obtain a long-term client, a reward greater than the single fee I might have expected in the beginning.

Step 5: Be a Hunter

I come from a long line of hunters. My late husband, sons, uncles, and cousins are all virtually gone from the moment hunting season opens until it ends. But trophy deer and bucks are not what I am referring to here. To get the "trophy" job, if you will, we have to do more, especially in a down market. Often, I consider myself blessed to have come into the recruiting business in the early eighties. It was a time when the market was extra tight, and we had to make forty to sixty cold calls per day. Whether you are a recruiter, applicant, or company HR representative, you will win the "golden trophy" if you go the extra mile—always. Applicants and candidates: if you are looking for a job in a tight market, or even in a good one, you owe it to yourself to look at all your options. And the only way to do so is to be a hunter. Recruiters and company representatives also must go on a hunt for the best talent. Now, I'm not implying that we need to interview hundreds of candidates, but make sure you get the trophy. Don't settle for less. Settle for *more*. And the only way to do so is to go on your own hunt, using the steps outlined in a later chapter of this book.

The Struggle to Change

I am an executive recruiter in one of the best and worst job markets in the country. I hear my clients talking constantly about the right experience, the right degree, and the right school, and if we don't find them, they don't want to take any action. It can be frustrating. My industry is very averse to change. The old regime doesn't want to listen to a new way of hiring people. They are stuck on the old model, even if the results they have been getting don't work.

But why not look at the whole person when we are trying to make a good hire? Even though doing so is logical, some employers are still resistant to this new model. Sometimes, they are willing to try it, but other times the jobs will go unfilled for months. But when experienced people are not available, alternative methods of hiring must be considered.

I work in an industry that is ruled at times by the "good ole boy" network. Oftentimes, I hear "it's my way or the highway; if you can't find me this person with exactly what I want, don't even think of presenting someone who has an entirely different skill set. I don't have time to train." But then I ask them, if the job has been open four times in the last two years, why not try something new? Is it cost effective to continue to pay recruiting fees because the people you are hiring don't stay on the job or are leaving for what they consider to be greener pastures. Sometimes, that gets their attention. But many times, they are still hesitant to do something they have never done before. Many companies and associate recruiters have not gotten on board. They would rather:

1. let jobs stay open for months and lose production;

2. make bad hires and blame it on internal challenges;

3. hire people who contribute little to the group but keep them on because they looked good on paper, graduated from a prestigious school, or seem to have promise;

4. match one piece of paper to another because that's the way recruiting has always been done; or

5. try not to rock the boat as an HR rep with a heavily tenured (usually generation X or baby boomer) supervisor.

I suppose as human beings, most of us are averse to change. But sometimes change is the only solution. Would you continue in a bad relationship if your needs are just not being met? Would you go back to the same restaurant if every time you ate there, the food was bad? Would you buy the same brand of shoes if they continued to pinch your toes? You get my drift. We all have our comfort zones, but sometimes comfort zones can be dangerous. We know what all the self-help books say about staying in our comfort zones: We don't grow. We stagnate. And it applies in business as well as in our personal lives.

But what if you had strong reasons to consider this method—a new way of hiring that would benefit all parties and make the hiring agent look like a superhero? Would you use a new hiring method that:

1. resulted in filling jobs in a timelier manner;

2. allowed the hiring agent to get a bigger bonus for doing a better job;

3. resulted in good hires who contributed more to the group, with longer retention and more promotions;

4. invited you to look under the hood of the resume, resulting in a stronger, better, and longer lived match; and

5. helped you understand generational differences in mindsets, allowing a blend of strengths and abilities to provide a more positive working environment and stronger morale among peers?

Sounds good, right?

Unfortunately, this industry is laden with old ways of doing business as it pertains to hiring employees. And many of them have been in the market in the down times when employees were plentiful. It's just not that way anymore. Times have changed. Significantly.

How do you teach an old dog new tricks? I've been asking myself this question a lot lately. Often it takes practicing with a dog over and over again before they finally learn it. I suppose the same rule applies for humans. Nothing worthwhile is ever easy, is it? I feel sure there are many good people in the job market who will be hired in the next year without the exact experience required. It's going to take some coaching and training on the part of recruiters to get clients to understand this new concept. It might take some time, but the results will be well worth the effort. Looking outside the box to solve problems is vital, and we can't let resistance or challenge stop us from our goals. Achievers never give up.

The Generational Mindset

Oftentimes, while doing placement work for my clients, I have an easier time with the millennials and digital natives getting on board with a new hiring method than baby boomers or those from generation X. And it's not that one generational mindset is better or worse, it's just that millennials are sometimes more open to new ideas or new ways of doing things than the traditional methods used for many years by the generation X folks.

When I talk to people about the skills gap and how we *must* consider alternative methods of hiring, their responses prove that they have not even considered what it's all about and the consequences that will arise if we don't start utilizing new methods now. If even the US Bureau of Labor Statistics is talking about the upcoming skills gap problem, it doesn't take a math major to understand that there will be a large lack of experienced workers to replace those retired folks. Something has to change. And some type of solution needs to be considered.

The Faremouth Method works in many situations. And the results are the same. It provides more solid placements, longer tenured employees, and people who are aligned with company cultures who eventually get promoted for their good work and contributions to advancing the bottom line. But we have to get folks to be open to it and to its many benefits.

If your leg is broken and you have to learn to walk again, it's not easy at first. However, the longer you do your therapy and overcome the challenges and discomfort, the more you can look forward to walking again. The old method of placing applicants is broken, and we need a new method to keep successful hires going forward in the future. Walking your way into more positive placement methods can be a wonderful experience for all involved. And those corporate and placement recruiters who start utilizing this method can start seeing results with a little practice.

Where Paper Meets People

The Faremouth Method engages both paper and people. The resume is only a starting point, but it is an important starting point nonetheless. A resume tells you many things. If it is well presented, without typos or bad grammar, it tells you the person took the time to present a product that reflects who they are. Also, it demonstrates a chronology of the applicant's achievements, work experiences, and tenure on the job.

But resumes, like all business documents, can be deceiving. Job seekers sometimes hire outside professionals to produce a resume for them, especially when they are changing jobs. As in all industries, I have seen a good deal of misrepresentation on resumes, and these inaccuracies are often only discovered when a recruiter meets with the job seeker in person. This is where the interviewer needs to employ their people skills to ask the correct questions to move past the resume.

When employers simply use a job board with a word search feature to screen applicants, they might not be able to accurately assess the applicant. The Faremouth Method utilizes both paper and people in the process of making successful hires. And when we use this method, everybody wins. The applicant is accurately assessed, given a chance to express their employment goals, and advised on available positions based on their background, personality, skills, and experience. They are also carefully informed about the culture of the company, as well as the job requirements, salary, benefits, vacation, etc. It's a win-win for all parties.

I. *Benefits to Businesses and Companies*

- Businesses can work with recruiters they rely on and trust.

- Applicants who are placed have a great deal to contribute to the company.

- Retention levels of candidates are up, and clients feel they are getting a new hire who is worth the recruiting fee and their investment of training.

- The HR rep or hiring supervisor of the department is more respected by their superior for making a good hire.

- Turnover costs are reduced, and the company gets a reputation for low turnover, which makes it a good place to work and attracts other candidates who want to work there.

- The company expands their profits by hiring competent, hardworking employees who have passion for their jobs.

2. *Benefits to the Applicant*

- The applicant is placed in a job they truly desire, and they look forward to going to work.

- Happier employees have stronger immune systems and often take less sick days.

- Well-placed employees, who report high job satisfaction, are happier at home and more likely to become better role models for younger family members.

- Satisfied employees are usually promoted more often than their less satisfied colleagues.

3. *Benefits to the Recruiter*

- Recruiters will get more referrals from both applicants and client companies, which will translate into productive placements and more profits.

- Other recruiters will want to work with successful recruiters and share jobs/profits.

- Recruiters who excel at using this method will create more lasting placements, which will translate to more referrals from vendors and associates.

CHAPTER 4

FOR THE RECRUITER

The Exceptional Recruiter

What makes a recruiter successful? "Effective recruiters know better than to judge a book by its cover or a candidate by their resume" (Pavlou 2017). Of course, a stellar professional resume can be presented, and a candidate may have taken some serious tutorials about how to interview. But an outstanding recruiter goes above and beyond. They dig deep into their subject and get under the hood of whatever their subject happens to be: a job order, a candidate, a new client company, or even an associate recruiter with whom they choose to share jobs.

Outstanding recruiters also "read between the lines and find proof that candidates' skills actually match the job requirements. Operational and behavioral interview questions can help identify qualified candidates" (Pavlou 2017). Recruiters that typically stand out are the ones who are innovative in their approach and applaud "the value of diversity over typical requirements. They suggest a candidate who they think is passionate enough to bring new ideas to their team, even if they don't come from a stereotypical background. Instead of hiring another 'beer buddy,' an effective recruiter will consider a candidate who's a 'culture add'—not a 'culture fit'" (Pavlou 2017).

Although all recruiters make placements, *exceptional* recruiters make placements that benefit applicant, recruiter, and client alike. The implementation of the five-step Faremouth Method is arguably the most efficient and successful process. This chapter thoroughly analyzes each step of this method, providing recruiters with the guidance necessary to successfully implement The Faremouth Method in their recruiting practice.

Being a recruiter these days can be challenging, and it's probably going to get harder in the near future. With the current shortage of available talent and the impending Gray Tsunami, recruiters are facing major challenges. The global aging challenge and shortage of qualified people in the workplace is, without a doubt, a reality. As a recruiter, you need to understand these real challenges, and it's important to have the skill set needed to assist your clients with their needs.

Step 1. Take Inventory

The first step in this process begins by reviewing your own methods and techniques. What methods have you used that worked for you? Do you assess the current market and who is hiring within it? Do you belong to professional organizations that allow you to grow and develop? Are you involved in continuing education programs that allow recruiters to become certified and recognized as accomplished in their fields? Do you strive to make a good match for all parties involved when making placements? Where can you improve in your technique? What can you do to make a name for yourself in your chosen area of recruiting? Are you taking advantage of the many features of LinkedIn, job boards, networking activities, etc., to get you into the flow of currently successful recruiting resources?

A recruiter also takes inventory of an applicant through the interview process. We do this by identifying the training classes, activities, and career experiences that the applicant most enjoyed. In addition, a recruiter can take inventory of a potential employer by researching a company's corporate culture. Visit the company to observe their culture, talk to employees and management, and gather as much information as possible.

Find the Story

Every applicant has a story. In fact, everything that leads them to your doorstep is part of their story, including their past training, successes, failures, passions, and motivations. As the interview process does not allow time for understanding an applicant's entire life story, the questions you ask are of paramount importance. You need to discern which aspects of their story will help you place them in the right job.

Corporations and businesses have stories as well. The business's creation, founders, growth, expansion, values, culture, current successes, needs, challenges, and concerns are as much a part of a company's story as its open positions and expectations about who should fill them. The client seeking to fill positions brings this vast and invisible story to the table when they contact you for applicants.

Step one of The Faremouth Method, the Self-Inventory, is where your prospective hires and your clients explain elements of their own story that they feel may be useful to you.

As recruiters, we must decide which elements of a personal or corporate story are useful to us. A successful placement benefits all parties: the applicant, the employer, and the recruiter. With an ideal placement, everybody wins.

Step 2. Ask Better Questions

When taking on new search projects, are you asking the right questions to understand your clients' needs? Are you visiting the clients to meet the people in the company so you can understand the culture of the company? When interviewing candidates, are you asking questions other than the traditional ones to get under the hood of the resume? Are you assessing skills, passions, accomplishments, and career goals and desires rather than only focusing on academic credentials and past experience?

Asking better questions helps recruiters delve into the personal or corporate story for critical information that will help them make a match.

When interviewing a prospective candidate, I start from the bottom of the resume and work my way to the present. I discern patterns that provide information about the candidate's ability to succeed in the respective job. Previous success and achievements are good indicators that a person will likely be successful in a new industry, product line, or new environment. A track record of past performance doing equally complex work is a far better predictor of success than checking boxes for skills or conducting a simple behavioral interview. The ability to solve realistic job-related problems is a great indicator of thinking skills, creativity, planning, and potential.

Use these same techniques to ask better questions of your clients. Carefully listening to the answers you receive is vital!

Three Strategies to Discover an Applicant's Skills and Passions

We are in changing times—times that force us to use different methods to solve our hiring problems. There is a real shortage of experienced talent available to hiring managers. And alternative methods of hiring must be implemented. How can we reduce the odds of making a bad hire when the candidates we are interviewing don't have the exact skill set we need for the jobs we are trying to fill?

The answer to this important question begins with the hiring authority having a clear understanding of what the job entails and clarifying expectations before the person is hired. If the interviewer clearly understands the mechanics of the job, then an accomplished high achiever can oftentimes transfer previous success to the task at hand.

Asking the right questions and observing previously demonstrated achievements can reduce the risk of making a bad hire.

Strategy #1: Discover the Patterns

At the onset of the interview, spend twenty to thirty minutes reviewing the candidate's background to determine a basic fit. Ask them the reasons they changed jobs and if the jobs were in alignment with their needs at the time. Changing jobs is a serious decision, so make sure their reasons are valid. Most importantly, make sure the person was at the top 30 percent of their peer group. This is the Accomplishment/Achiever Pattern.

Some clues may be:

- consistent evidence of moving up the ladder, including promotions, raises, and achievement awards;

- always seeking more challenging job duties compared to their peer group;

- seeking out "not in my job description" assignments that others chose not to do, which broadened their base of professional and personal growth; or

- markers of achievement, such as recognition awards, increasing sales dramatically, or cost-saving corporate methods that translated into higher efficiency for the company.

Strategy #2: Discover What They Are Proud Of

Ask the applicant to describe the accomplishment they were most proud of in each of their last few jobs and observe the trend of performance over time. It's helpful to make a specific evaluation of their fit by comparing their accomplishments to the job description's requirements for productivity.

Strategy #3: Ask about Problem Solving

Ask the candidate how they would figure out a hypothetical problem and what strategies they would utilize to solve it. Give them a real problem your client has encountered and ask them how their previous experience would have prepared them to solve it. Also ask how some similarities in the previous challenges would relate to the tasks they would be encountering in the new role.

Conducting a performance-based interview is a direct approach. It all starts by knowing what the person hired needs to do to be considered successful. As a result, you will discover the clarifying expectations before the person is hired. This is the secret to not only great hiring but also great management.

It has to be a win-win for all. You want a top performer to want to work for your client, but you want to make sure his previous achievements and accomplishments align well with your client's goals and direction. Making a good hire in these changing times takes a new approach. It takes a bit more time to utilize this method, but the results are well worth the effort and lead to strong retention and expanded growth for the applicant and the company.

Seven Interview Questions

Often, candidates enter my office unsure of what they want to do. They could be looking for their first job out of college, or stuck in a job that doesn't fulfill their needs. Other times, the rug is pulled out from under them and they have lost a job or are affected by a change in their company. Below are some of the specific questions I ask to learn the valuable information I need to lead the candidate in the right direction and help them find a career or job that is in alignment with who they are.

My experience with an applicant by the name of Dexter demonstrates my methods and questions. Dexter was an impressive young man who came to me after he received his bachelor's degree in business. He was confused about his career path and was frustrated that he had had many interviews but none that had turned out in his favor. He was an ambitious young man and had worked full time while attending college. He had paid for his entire education and graduated with a 3.7 GPA. In high school, Dexter was the president of Junior Achievement and led his division to a national competition. He was self-confident and smart, and he had extremely good verbal skills.

As always, I began our interview with questions about the past and moving forward. It is the details of these answers that help me determine the applicant's skills, interests, and abilities. I knew early on that Dexter was a driven young man who enjoyed challenge and growth. However, knowing just that wasn't enough. I needed to dig deeper to assess what type of career would be fulfilling for him and allow him to thrive. Here is a list of my questions, Dexter's answers, and how I determined what career path would allow this young man to find a career he would enjoy:

1. *"Tell me about the classes you enjoyed in school and the reason you decided on a business curriculum in college."*
    "I enjoyed my finance classes and the classes that allowed me to investigate ideas and theories."

2. *"What was it about those classes that challenged you and made them interesting?"*
    "I like to investigate and find the needle in the haystack. I enjoy doing research and acting like a detective through investigative work."

3. *"What duties in your college jobs were the most fulfilling for you and why?"*
    "I worked for a mortgage broker and had to investigate many issues to ensure there were no liens on titles or bad debts. I had to do all the background investigative work for the owner before he closed the deal. I enjoyed the research associated with that."

4. *"What aspects of your previous jobs did you least enjoy, and why?"*
    "I didn't like dealing with the complaining customers or enduring their dissatisfaction when my information didn't match what they had provided. I much prefer the investigative work and doing the back-end duties as opposed to countering objections."

5. *"What single project or task would you consider your most significant accomplishment in your career or education to date?"*
    "I enjoyed being the president of Junior Achievement. We handled a project from conception to completion. We worked as a team to bring our product to market. I also liked being mentored by senior level executives. I liked dealing with the

presidents of companies and receiving their guidance. To be able to compete in a national competition was also a big thrill for me."

6. *"With what kind of people do you most enjoy interacting? Also, do you like a formal or casual environment in the workplace?"*
"I like being around successful people who have worked hard and succeeded in their career. I like to dress up. I wouldn't like a place where I had to wear jeans."

7. *"If you could do any job you wanted, what would you do and why?"*
"I would run a company, have a huge office, and live in a penthouse suite. I would have a lot of responsibility and surround myself with smart, competent people."

These answers showed me the type of career Dexter would enjoy. I needed to find a job with finance and research components, a professional environment, and strong potential for growth.

A national insurance company had an open risk manager trainee position. They needed a smart person able to investigate the company's risk situation and assess the type of coverage necessary to protect them from financial loss. After an initial two-hour interview, the company immediately made Dexter an offer and increased the starting salary significantly in order to match his outstanding skill set. Dexter has been in this job for almost a year now, and both Dexter and the company are happy. Dexter interacts daily with senior executives, has boardroom meetings, and receives mentoring from respected executives.

Step 3. Step Out of Your Comfort Zone

If you have always done recruiting the traditional way, are you willing to consider alternative methods? Have you tried to think outside of the box? When a client gives you tight specs, are you willing to try to convince them that what they think they need to hire might not be the only profile they should consider? Have you ever tried to understand a candidate and suggest alternative career paths for them that might work better than what they told you they wanted to do? Have you ever tried to develop an area of specialization that might be more in demand than your current area of expertise in recruiting? If you always placed people in the medical field, for example, have you considered working in the robotic field, where the same technical screening skills may be required? Such a field might be an up-and-coming area that needs recruiters and will have a demand for hiring through a third party.

My professional affiliates frequently complain about the struggle to find quality, experienced candidates. But they often search for these candidates in the wrong places, searching only for specifically experienced people with straightforward resumes. Given the shortage of talent, such candidates may not exist. As recruiters, we must implement alternative methods of hiring and educate our clients on the advantages of hiring a new breed of employees. We must think outside the box to tap into resources that might be foreign to traditional hiring methods. The right companies and candidates exist; we just need to use a different kind of net to catch these new fish.

Step 4. Take Your Time and Do It Right

As recruiters, many of us do not get paid until a position is filled. However, that's no reason for us to rush the process and just throw resumes at a position; that wouldn't ensure a good hire, would it? As a recruiter, are you taking the time to get to know the client, the applicant, and their specific demands and requirements to make a good match? Or are you simply looking at a job description and a resume and finding keywords that match? I saw a national news show once that discussed a new job board that had been created. The newscaster had asked, "Well, how do you know the information on the profile is honest and true? Can't people lie on these about many things?" And he was right. Take the time to check your facts on both parties and make sure you have the correct information to make a good match. Taking a little more time to make the placement can ensure a good placement, and many referrals from both the candidate and the applicant can result from a good hire.

Because of the challenge of our current job market, there is a great deal of motivation for recruiters to speed up and automate a process that should take a good investment of time and energy. Of course, we need good websites, professional staffs, and a simple, streamlined process for gathering resumes, contacts, and job listings. But resist the urge to rush past the human-to-human interactions. Real, focused conversations and interviews have the best chance of bringing you matches and placements that benefit all parties. That is also where you build your reputation as a professional who listens and matches people to people, not just as a recruiter who matches paper to paper.

Step 5. Be a Hunter

The hunter mentality is not just limited to candidates. Recruiters must be hunters too. Even if you are a seasoned recruiter, you cannot expect the clients or applicants to come to you. You have to be proactive. Continuing to make marketing calls and providing interesting blogs or articles for candidates allows you to gather more prospects into your business pipeline.

You must be committed to improving your craft, not just sitting stagnant. The only constant in life is change, so why would our industry not be ever-changing, as well? To be the best you can be, you must seek to improve. Enroll in continuing education courses in your fields and search out new sources of information to provide your candidates with the best service possible.

Also, try giving back on occasion; getting out into the community demonstrates that you are committed to your career and industry. Even consider volunteering on committees to help various people find jobs. Back in 2008, when we were in recession and many people were losing jobs, I volunteered at a jobs ministry with many other seasoned professionals. To this day, I still get

THE FAREMOUTH METHOD

referrals from those contacts. And going after something that didn't bring an immediate return brought me greater respect from my peers within the industry. Being a hunter—being proactive—is important as a recruiter. Also, stay up-to-date with rules and regulations, technology, etc.; this can help you connect with others who may have techniques and needs different from your own.

Be assertive and look for candidates in places other recruiters may not be looking. In this compressed job market, you may find that you need to step out of your home industry and begin helping folks place candidates in adjacent or related fields. Don't wait for the right clients or candidates to come to you; use your networks and your communities, stay active on social media and web-based portals, and keep building your business—one friendship, one colleague, one conference, one successful placement at a time.

Ten Tasks for the Exceptional Recruiter

If you have decided to pursue a career as a professional recruiter, congratulations! You have a vital job; you can help a candidate advance their career, help an employer solve a difficult hiring situation, or help an associate recruiter find a good candidate for a difficult match. You can help or hurt a lot of people by what you do, and because of this, it's important that you continue on this career path for the right reasons.

There are two different types of recruiters: *retained search* recruiters and *contingency search* recruiters. They have essentially the same goal but different types of contracts with their employers. A retained search recruiter gets paid whether they fill the job or not. Contingency search recruiters are what their title says, their fee is contingent on them filling a job.

Thirty years as a recruiter has taught me that certain qualities allow us as recruiters to assist many in the task of making successful placements and to have professional careers we can be proud of. Always remember to:

1. keep honesty and integrity the foundation of your practice;

2. join professional organizations to keep current with your industry and professional practices;

3. seek out other recruiters you value and trust to broaden your base and to increase your placement volume;

4. take continuing education programs and become certified to gain reputation among your peers;

5. do your homework to understand your clients' needs and your applicants' goals, and ask for referrals from both segments;

6. keep your professional and personal lives separate, but be mindful, even in your own personal connections, that your behavior is always being held to a professional standard;

7. keep up-to-date with technology, social media, and other current platforms;

8. understand how to market/advertise to generational market segments, i.e. know what a millennial would respond to in an ad as opposed to what a baby boomer would;

9. value your relationships with other recruiters, clients, and applicants; and

10. make sure you give back—involve yourself in volunteer, community-service activities.

The Impatient Bartender

A few years ago, I met an impressive young woman named Terri. She came highly recommended to me by a person who regularly sends me extremely good candidates. Over the years, I have placed most of the candidates recommended by my friend into good, high-paying jobs. But in Terri's case, even though she impressed me, I chose not to place her at all.

Terri was one of the most personable young women I had interviewed in a long time. I had placed most of Terri's friends in the oil and gas industry, and she was enthusiastic about jumping on this bandwagon. She had a burning desire to get into the industry in a sales capacity. Most of her friends were doing extremely well and making high salaries. Terri had been tending bar at night for the last few years and was going to school during the day. She had already completed three years of college toward a bachelor's degree in business. She told me she was making $60K as a bartender and wanted to stop going to school and get into the oil and gas business. I sat back in my desk chair, looked at this young woman, and asked, "Why do you want to do that? You are so close to getting your degree. Why would you throw all that hard work down the drain?" She told me she would go back at some point and finish her degree, but for now she wanted an oil and gas job. To her surprise, I told her that getting a job now was not the smartest thing to do. With no experience in the industry, she would be lucky to get a salary of $40–$45K. It might take her two to three years to even get to the $60K range, and if she did that or better, she would probably never go back to school. Since she was paying for her own education without student loans, the lower salary would make it more difficult to finish her degree. I also told her that, with a degree in business, she would become a more marketable candidate in the industry. I don't mean to suggest that a degree is mandatory for success for every person. But this young woman was obviously a good student, maintaining a 3.5 GPA while working. She liked going to school and told me she enjoyed learning. I suggested she keep the bartender job and register for the next semester. I also told her that a degree is a big indicator to a prospective employer that you are willing not only to start something but to see it through to completion. Having only three years of college on a resume isn't anywhere near as impressive as a degree. And leaving so close to graduation might encourage prospective employers to doubt her ability to stick with something.

Of course, there are exceptions to every rule. We all know Bill Gates, Michael Dell, and many others with famous success stories were people who didn't get a degree. But in Terri's case, I didn't quite see her in that same category. And I could have focused on my own self-gain as a recruiter and pushed her into a sales job at $40K; I would have made a fee and posted another placement on my books. But would that have been the right thing to do for Terri and my employer? If Terri got in there at a lower salary, especially when her lifestyle for the last several years had been on a much higher level, would she stay in the job? If she didn't, how would that make the employer feel? If she left the job within a short amount of time, would it look like I make solid placements? Would the employer continue to call me for future jobs?

Terri walked out of my office with a plan. And while I spent over an hour of my time interviewing her, the investment of time was well worth it. She went out to dinner with her friends that night and sent me three good candidates whom I could place. She keeps in touch with me and tells me that when she does get her degree, she will call me. So often, the rewards of good efforts come to us in indirect ways.

Broaden Your Goals

Every applicant has a story. And we as recruiters must decide if their story is one we can do something with. A placement should serve all parties: the applicant, the employer, and the recruiter. If handled correctly, everybody wins.

As a recruiter, don't get discouraged if you don't place every single person who comes into your office. If you give the right advice for all concerned, the rewards will always come back to you. The goal should be not only to place candidates, but to form lasting professional relationships that will benefit all parties over time. This will require you to broaden your goals for what you do and how you do it. Understanding the applicant's story is crucial to being able to make the right assessment on the course of action to take. It feels good when you help another person in your community grow and develop. Understanding what the applicant needs is vital in serving their best interests.

Top Five Mistakes Recruiters Make

Recruiters in general get a bad rap. Most people don't care to work with them, whether they are an HR representative for a company, an applicant or candidate seeking job placement assistance, or an associate network recruiter. Shake them all up in the bag, and the result you usually get is frustration, anxiety, and not a good experience.

There are of course exceptions to this rule, and of course there are good recruiters out there. But why does recruitment, as a profession, get put in the negative category?

In thinking through the answers to this question, there aren't any one-size-fits-all answers. In most cases, it depends on whether the recruiter is dealing with a company, candidate, or associate recruiter. But overall, the general reasons they are seen negatively have to do with the top five mistakes recruiters make:

1. Recruiters sometimes put their fee (or yearly bonus) first instead of last. Most recruiters don't get paid until they fill a position. There is usually a sense of urgency to fill a job so they can make a placement and get paid. Most of the recruiters who work on a contingency basis don't get paid until the candidate gets placed, as opposed to retained search recruiters, who get paid a portion of the fee up front. Retained search recruiters are usually only retained for executive-type searches, however. If the fee is the recruiter's primary goal, it's not seen to be in the best interest of the recruiter to take the time to get to know the company or the candidate. They take what the client tells them at face value, look at a resume, and make a match. They don't take the time to do it right.

2. Although many recruiting and staffing professionals these days are certified, there are a limited number of

continuing education courses available concerning the current market and the skills gap. There are different types of recruiters, but in most cases they are salespeople. And as we know, a salesperson's main job is to sell their product. Also, most recruiters are not trained or educated about global generational differences and, therefore, do not communicate these market changes to the hiring authorities.

3. Many recruiters don't take full advantage of professional organizations related to their profession or industry specialization. They don't consider attending conventions, conferences, or continuing education courses in order to remain current on the conditions of the market, nor do they consider the networking opportunities provided by such events.

4. Recruiters often don't think outside the box, and many recruiters only consider traditional methods of hiring that may not work in today's marketplace.

5. Many recruiters keep their head in the sand about changing times. They don't take into consideration generational differences and different global mindsets—that is, are they talking to a generation X or baby boomer employer who wants to hire a millennial or digital native as a worker? If so, do they take the time to educate all parties on the different mindsets early on so there is an understanding up front of the generational differences among coworkers? Or do they try to shove a millennial's mindset down the throat of someone from generation X who just can't comprehend *why* the millennial won't do the job the way it has always been done?

Recruiters need to follow companies like Google, Facebook and Yahoo, who take into consideration our changing work environment. To survive as a recruiter in the future workplace, they must get on board and take note of the many changes facing us all.

The Man with a House to Build

Despite being a recruiter for many years, I have never stopped learning. I find it wonderful that, even with all my experience and training, I continue to learn new lessons about the difference between needs and wants for both candidates and employers. Recently, I had an opportunity to remember just how important listening is. I had an applicant named Ted. Ted was a racehorse candidate who had all the ingredients of a successful placement, I had placed him twice in the last fifteen years, and I thought I knew this young man and what his needs were. Well, as we all know, people are a variable product and their needs change. Ted had an MBA and a successful career as a sales representative, in which he had progressed up the ranks to vice president. I had always felt Ted had the right stuff for him to be promoted to president of a company, if he was positioned correctly in the right organization. I even had a job listing on my desk that had the potential to allow Ted to move into such a role.

Ted had been with his last company for seven years when a new president came in. The new president let all the senior management go and brought in his own team to handle the executive-level positions. Ted was given a nice severance package and called me to place him in another job. When he told me what he was looking for, he also told me he couldn't take a huge pay cut as he was in the process of building a new home. He said he had started the plans before he left his current job and was in too deep to reverse the process. He had already put a lot of money into this project, and they had already broken ground.

Nevertheless, I presented Ted with the available posting, a job at a director level that would eventually replace the company president, who would be retiring in a few years. The starting salary was somewhat lower than what Ted had been making, but the potential for advancement was huge. His salary would easily be doubled, just not right away. I sent Ted on the interview for the director role, and the president loved him.

He knew what Ted had been making but wanted to start him out at a somewhat lower salary, as Ted didn't have experience directly related to the industry and he would have to learn the product. Ted would have to learn the market segment and establish new relationships, but his skills were transferrable, and I knew he could learn what he needed to in a short amount of time. He had had no industry-related experience going into his last role but had taken the company to amazing profits that they had never had before. We worked out a trial period for him to examine the role and products, and we all knew it would be a test experience.

While I had high hopes that it would work, it didn't. Looking back, I realize that we failed because I hadn't listened to what the candidate needed. He asked me to find him a job with a salary line commensurate with his last job. That's what he needed, and he needed it right now. The red flags were all over the place, but I was focusing on Ted's ability to advance, his training, and his qualifications—who he was in the past. I wasn't looking at who he was today, and I lost my focus on what he needed right now. What he needed right now was a salary that would allow him to handle his current financial obligation.

For Ted, the ability to make a huge salary in years to come wouldn't do the trick. Potential was not as important an ingredient in the mix. I wasn't listening, and it quickly came back to haunt me. I went for about a week without hearing from him, and when I checked in with him, I found out he had received an offer from a previous customer who paid a bit more than he had been making in his job of seven years. The company, from Europe, was opening an office here in the United States and needed a racehorse to get their new division off the ground. The chance for Ted to be president would probably never happen with the company, which was a family business that filled all senior management positions through their internal framework of people. But Ted wasn't focused on potential then. His focus was on being able to afford his big investment and not losing all the money he had already put down. He didn't have the luxury to wait for a big-cheese role of president down the road.

Ted was a heavy reminder that I needed to look at the whole person and focus on who they are right now, not simply on a resume or past accomplishments. It was an expensive lesson for me, but my mother always told me some of the best lessons in life are those that are the toughest and end up costing us something, whether financially, emotionally, or physically.

Make sure you listen to your candidate and don't focus on the past. If you don't, it could cost you big time. I'm sure my ears are going to be extra sharp in the future! This was a good lesson, and it firmly drove the message of this book into me. Listen to your applicant and focus on who they are today, not on what they were in the past and what you want their needs to be. Their needs *right now* should be top priority.

Understanding the Employer

Have you ever had a challenging employer you needed to figure out? It can be frustrating to be unsure of what an employer wants in a candidate, and that uncertainty can often result in a job going unfilled. Increasing your placement success numbers requires that you make sure you understand your client and send him the best candidates for the job. It's all about being thorough and taking the time to ask the right questions.

When I get a new client who is local, I usually ask to visit the client's business. If I happen to know most of the people in the company from years of attending conferences and conventions, or I have worked with them through hiring authorities at other companies, it isn't as crucial for me to go to the site. But in many cases, I usually ask the HR rep or hiring authority if I can visit the site. Doing this tells me many things. It puts me in close contact with the culture of the company. It lets me see the physical work area and gives me a much better idea of who would fit into the company. Also, it usually bonds me to the client company and reassures the client that I have a vested interest in their success. It often takes a chunk out of my day to do this, but it is always worth the time and effort. I also ask the hiring authority as much as I can about successful and not-so-successful employees to glean what the important characteristics of an applicant would be. Just the other day, a new client asked me if a prospective candidate played golf. That was important to the president. All the successful sales reps did, and it seemed to work well with entertaining their most valuable clients.

Also, to understand the client and to be extremely good at recruiting, you need to understand your market and coach and educate the client. Often, I have clients call in a job order and tell me what they *think* they need but give me a salary range that is much lower than market standards. These are typically clients who have been in senior management roles for many years and have no real understanding of current market conditions. They think doing it the same way they have done their searches in the past will be successful. Times are much different now, and they need to understand that. There is a shortage of qualified candidates available, and being creative on my end has proven to increase my ratio of jobs filled.

Just recently, I had a client who was the VP of a manufacturing facility call me and tell me he needed an inside sales and proposals analyst for a pipe mill. What this job required was a person who was detail-oriented, had strong Excel skills, and could interface with many different vendors, customers, and internal people in this company. Any knowledge of pipe manufacturing would have been a plus, but as this was a specific type of pipe, there were few people available with direct experience. I counseled the client and repeated back to him what my understanding was of the job. I told him that to find a candidate with every requirement he was telling me he needed might be a challenge. There were few of those types of candidates available, and those who were, were only available at a premium. I asked him if he had a training program in place, and he told me he did have people available to train the new person. I suggested we see a variety of candidates with directly related and unrelated experience. He agreed, and I sent him three candidates.

All these candidates were outstanding in their own way and had proven experience and references that convinced me they were capable of doing the job. I also felt they would all fit with the culture of the company, as this was a long-standing client of mine and I had been to the facility many times. I had placed many people at this company in the past, so I was familiar with the culture and who would fit in. A candidate who fits in with the rest of the group is an important ingredient in the mix. If you have a qualified candidate who has exact experience, but the personalities and culture are not a solid match, the chances are high that, despite being capable for the job, they won't be happy in the day-to-day interaction with the group and might not stay in the long run. Retention has always been important to me when I make a placement. It also makes the client happy, and they consider the services I provide a good investment. After the client interviewed the three candidates, he called me and told me he liked them all. He couldn't decide which one to hire, and he needed another manager in the company to meet the people and help him decide. We set each of them up for a second interview.

The person he ended up hiring had related experience, had been in her last job over eight years, had solid Excel skills, and had much in common with the direct supervisor in the department. They offered her the job, and she accepted. The client told me he was also trying to find a place for the other two in the company, as he liked their skill sets and felt they would fit in.

As a recruiter, you must refine your list of questions to ask the client; the answers to these will provide a good road map to follow when screening your candidates. You need to get under the hood of the job order and ask probing questions of your client. Also, I can't stress enough how you must coach and counsel the clients as to current market conditions. If you don't advise them correctly, you could go in circles and, worse yet, end up not filling the job. Take the time to get all the information you need on the front-end. Also, know the culture of the company and the type of people who have been successful in the past. Ask questions, coach the client, and be thorough in your reference checks. Taking the extra time on the front-end could save you much time in the recruiting process. Time is money in our business. Use your time wisely, and it will provide you with a lucrative recruiting practice.

The Recruiter Reinvention

If you have been a recruiter for any length of time, you know that things are always changing. We constantly need to reinvent ourselves. When I got into this business in 1982, all we had was a phone and a phone book to assist us with getting clients and applicants. We didn't have any computers, job boards, iPads, or smart phones. We essentially had to roll up our sleeves, do a lot of tedious research, and get on the phone and make lots of marketing cold calls. I suppose you can tell that I am a baby boomer and that the way we did things back then, and even now, is much different from all the technological advances we have to work with these days. But when I compare how I got started and how I do things today, one thing remains the same. The human element, no matter how you slice it, is an important variable. It raises its head in many discussions, techniques, and interviews about recruiting. And it needs to be factored in when we hire.

The Faremouth Method offers tips for the recruiter to allow an accurate assessment to take place. Technology is a helpful tool in handling recruiting requirements. But if we only rely on technology and miss the human element, the chances of making a match beneficial to all parties are diminished.

A Blending of Old and New

The traditional methods of recruiting aren't working. I hear it all the time. Just the other day, the HR rep of a large international conglomerate remarked to me, "You are really good at what you do. You had strong competition on this job order, and again you beat out a large national staffing agency. We are all amazed at your track record. What do you do that continues to allow you to fill all our staffing needs?"

I told her I had a method of recruiting that is an alternative method. It's not rocket science. Essentially, it's a blending of old and new methods that keeps the human element at the center of what I do. But competition in my field is at an all-time high. The scarcity of jobs and the huge numbers of recruiters available to fill these jobs are causes for serious concern. If recruiters are not willing to reinvent themselves and take a good hard look at the challenges in the marketplace of today, jobs will be filled by those who do reinvent themselves. We are living in a different recruiting world. In most cases, traditional methods of hiring are not getting jobs filled and, more importantly, don't allow the companies high retention.

The mindsets of millennials and generation X workers are different. And employees these days are looking for a different work experience. For several years leading up to the time of this writing, *Fortune* magazine has ranked Google as number one on their list of "100 Best Companies to Work For," because Google has a real understanding of today's workers. If HR representatives and, more importantly, third party recruiters are not aware of this changing trend and *informing* their corporate hiring authorities of these changes in worker mindsets, they are not allowing a solid placement to take place.

Every company will differ in their culture, corporate mindset, and practices. But if the recruiter handling a job order doesn't have a method that understands both the company culture and the employee's needs, and an understanding of current market conditions, their chances of making the placement are slim to none. Also, we now live in a world of high technology. And in many ways, it increases our efficiency in what we all do and how we live. However, relying totally on digital measures to match a person to a job, without some ingredient of the human element present, usually won't produce a successful and lasting outcome in a placement.

There are many variables to consider in making a placement in today's market. As recruiters, we need to be aware of what the climate is in our area of expertise and how we might have to diversify to stay productive.

But let's consider a recent experience I had that successfully allowed me to make a solid placement and beat out my competition, who had a higher chance of filling the job because of their resources. Their up-to-date technology and the digital practices of today's world should have given them a strong advantage. So, what went wrong for them; why did they not fill the job? Below is an illustration of the steps I took to handle this search assignment. This is not an all-inclusive recipe for every job order that comes across a recruiter's desk. But it worked for this case, and many before it, and may well be worth your consideration.

The HR representative called me in need of someone to fill a highly technical position at her company. She gave me a timeline for when the person was leaving and told me that it was critical this position be filled as soon as possible. As it wasn't a position I fill every single day, I had to be extremely creative in my process:

1. In beginning this search, I had to take the time to visit the client and make sure I understood the corporate culture of the company. I also had to be aware of whether I had the resources to fill such a position totally on my own. To do so, I needed to find answers to the following questions:
    - What types of people made up the department?
    - What were the backgrounds of the people in the department—education, experience, mindset?
    - What were the values of the corporate culture?
    - Was the salary the client told me they wanted to pay realistic with the requirements and skills required to do the job in this current market?
    - What was the pulse of this company, and what were the variables of the most successful candidates?

2. If this job order required a highly technical candidate, were my resources alone sufficient to fill this job in a timely manner?
    - Was collaboration with a specialist in my network a step I needed to take?
    - With the downturn in the market in this industry, where would these types of candidates display their profiles? Was LinkedIn, or other social media, a good starting place, or did I need to dig deeper into who in the marketplace may have let people go?

3. Knowing I had a big firm as my competition, what did I need to do to compete and stay in the race? Was it even worth my efforts when my competition had fifteen recruiters, a database full of highly technical candidates, and a national reputation that intimidated the most successful independent recruiter?
   - Did I need to reflect back on my own personal track record of success with this company?
   - Did I need to put the fear in the trash can and believe in my abilities and passion to deliver good service and fulfill my clients' needs?
   - Did I need to work faster, longer, and as efficiently as possible to produce solid candidates?
   - Although I needed to work fast, how I could ensure that I would not work sloppily and simply refer to the client a resume that had all the buzzwords?

4. Was my brand image such that it would impress a candidate or company of this caliber enough for them to want to work with me?
   - What steps had I taken to make sure I could project the correct image for these types of candidates to want an independent to represent them as opposed to a large national agency?
   - Did I have the reputation, accreditations, and integrity established to attract qualified candidates? As a recruiter, was I up-to-date with what these types of workers responded to?
   - Was a revamp of my website necessary to project the necessary brand that would attract and retain clients and candidates?

5. Had I done my homework sufficiently on both sides of the equation to totally understand the client and applicant needs?
   - Did I take the time to counter objections from both parties?

- Was an in-person meeting, Skype, or video teleconference more appropriate to evaluate applicant responses than only speaking with them over the phone?
- Did I ask the necessary questions to gather outside-the-box information that was legally and professionally appropriate to ensure a good match?

In the end, we secured an outstanding candidate, the offer was made, and the candidate accepted. All parties were pleased, and a start date was arranged. In utilizing steps that blended technology and digital services with the human element, we were able to make a solid placement. The use of social networks and other digital profiles, such as candidate search tools, has opened up much wider talent pools for recruiters to utilize. However, while digital tools are here to stay, they will never fully replace the human instinct necessary for identifying the right candidates.

Five Traits that Separate a *Great* Recruiter from a *Good* One

If you take the time to speak to recruiters who have garnered a reputation for success, you will discover that they share a few traits in common. As a recruiter, if you strive to emulate these common interests, inclinations, and skills, then you can add the most value to your interactions with clients and candidates and stand out among your peers as a *great* recruiter.

Trait #1: Great at Networking

Zig Ziglar once said, "You can get everything in life you want if you will just help enough other people get what they want" (quoted in Eha 2012). And I believe that to be true. When you, as a recruiter, have a sincere interest in your client company or candidate's well-being and put it before your own, good matches will take place. Attend conventions and conferences to conduct networking and keep abreast of the current market conditions. Go the extra mile—not only to make good placements but to make connections with others in your industry and the community. If you can, give speeches, seminars, or training sessions, which will demonstrate to others your interest in people. Kevin Wheeler (2011), a well-known consultant, writes that "all solid relationships are built on quid pro quo: doing something for someone who, in turn, does something for you. It is this give and take that makes for success," and you must be "willing to share [your] career advice, mentoring skills, and technical expertise. In return," you will get "the loyalty and commitment" of client companies and candidates.

Trait #2: Strong Persuasive Skills and Marketing Ability

A great recruiter is a good listener. Listen intently to your candidate's thoughts and desires about a career move, and use your persuasive skills to counter any objections the client or company may have. Only when you understand the needs of others can you sincerely influence your customers. A great recruiter should also know the client well enough to market a good candidate with valuable experience to a prospective client company, even if the client does not have a current need. Demonstrate how a candidate can bring solid benefits to a client company, and you can often make a placement that otherwise would not have taken place.

Trait #3: Personalizing and Leveraging Uniqueness

Great recruiters utilize the power of personalization. Know how to form a bond with both client companies and applicants to steer the right candidates to the right hiring authorities. Take the time to gather deep knowledge of all parties through investigation and networking. Through your fact-finding sessions, you can ensure a solid placement that ensures long-term retention.

Trait #4: Using Technology without Dependency

Whether you are a millennial or a baby boomer, you should know how to blend technology with the human element. There are many mobile apps (such as LinkedIn, Facebook Page Manager, and

Indeed) that allow recruiters to both post job openings and search for candidates right from their smart phones. However, don't just use keyword searches and don't just conduct phone interviews. Take the time to get more information on the candidate to assure they will be a good match for your client company.

Trait #5: Staying In Touch after the Decision Is Made

When you stay in touch with both the candidates and the clients after the hiring decision has been made, you bond with them. Take interest in the growth and development of all parties involved. Take the time to visit customers after the placements are made and even during times when hiring is light. Oftentimes, happy candidates will refer friends to you, and your clients will often send their vendors or customers to you for additional business.

Great recruiters are determined to get results, but what should be most important is that both the client and the candidate feel they have had a real exchange and that both have benefited from the recruiter's involvement in the placement. Put candidates and clients first, and you will make not only solid placements but solid contacts for future growth.

The Landscape Designer

When a recruiter seeks to understand the job seeker, they must also strategize how to transfer a candidate's degrees, fields of study, qualifications, and work history into other fields. We are all on our own personal quest, our own personal journey. Finding the right destination, however, may be more difficult for some than for others. When we graduate from high school and pursue an area of study, the degree we receive after four years of hard work may not be easily marketable. After we graduate, market conditions change, business climates change, and here we are with a degree that is not in high demand. A degree in business, marketing, finance, accounting, or engineering will usually stand the test of time. But if your candidate received a degree with limited opportunity in the current market segment, what can you, as a recruiter, do?

The question I am asked by many candidates goes something like this: "How do I transfer my degree, area of study, or qualifications into a job in today's market? I want a job with purpose and fulfillment." The Faremouth Method allows me to be creative and look at the whole person I am interviewing. In the old method, a recruiter might have answered with "I can't help you. Go back to school," or something else along the lines of politely telling them their situation is hopeless and they can't find a solution to their important quest. But with the new method, solutions can be found. The interviewer should be able to identify the candidate's purpose, the factor that will align them to a real job currently available in the market. To discover this, you must ask a series of questions. If you use the old method and simply ask the candidate "What do you really want to do?", they will often tell you about fantasy jobs that are not grounded in reality.

Henrietta was a candidate of mine who drove home this point. Henrietta had received a degree in agricultural business. On her resume, she listed courses taken to include:

1. Fruit & Vegetable Production;

2. Integrated Pest Management; and

3. Landscape Design.

If I chose to only utilize conventional methods of hiring, I probably would have put this resume in the file labeled *Not Placeable*. Instead, I used an exercise that gave me valuable information and allowed me to give Henrietta hope and a plan of action:

Mary Ann: What classes did you most enjoy in high school and college?

Henrietta: I really enjoyed math and science.

Mary Ann: What percentage ranking did you receive in your graduating class?

Henrietta: I was at the top 4 percent.

Mary Ann: Why did you decide to pursue a degree in agricultural business?

Henrietta: My parents own an A/C business, and I've been around business all my life. I decided to get a degree in agricultural business because I like learning about things to do with the earth.

Mary Ann: Did you take any computer classes in college?

Henrietta: I did, and I am at advanced levels. (Testing demonstrated this to be true.)

Mary Ann: What was your GPA in college?

Henrietta: I graduated with a 3.66 GPA.

Mary Ann: What work experience or internships have you had that you most enjoyed?

Henrietta: I really enjoyed my internship in France at a winery. I maintained the fields and handled sophisticated reports on Excel spreadsheets. I loved working in the field, interacting with the workers, and being part of the team. I also liked working with the irrigation process in the field. The Department of Agricultural Sciences is also aligned with the Engineering Technology Department, so I studied irrigation classes in school and was able to understand the process at the winery. I liked the engineering aspects of the job.

Mary Ann: Why haven't you looked into going to work for another winery?

Henrietta: It was a nice experience, but coming back to Houston, I want to work in the oil and gas industry.

Mary Ann: What jobs or internships did you least enjoy?

Henrietta: I hated the job at the graphics company where I was simply a secretary and had to sit behind a desk.

Mary Ann: What experiences have you had that you are most proud?

Henrietta: I'm proud that I was able to go to France, adapt to a totally new culture, and make a contribution. That really fulfilled me.

Mary Ann: If you had a magic wand and you could be anything, what would it look like?

Henrietta: I would be working in the oil and gas business, with a technical component to the job, where I could move around, work with my hands, and work with a team.

Mary Ann: What is the biggest challenge you have faced in your life up until this point, and how did you handle it?

Henrietta: My parents really wanted me to take over the family business someday. The money is good, but it's not something I want to do. I have been able to convince them that I need to do what I know is right for me, not what they want me to do.

Mary Ann: If you had to give me your top three priorities in a job, with number one being the most important, what would they be?

Henrietta: (1) Work in the oil and gas business, where I could move around and do something with the earth, or an offshoot of that process; (2) have potential for growth; and (3) money.

After receiving the answers to these questions, I shared with the applicant what I had gleaned of her desires from the interview:

1. To work in the oil and gas business
2. To move around in her job, have opportunity for growth, and earn a healthy salary
3. To work in a job where she had a chance to see processes from inception to completion
4. To have a job where she would be mentally challenged
5. To use her strong computer skills

She told me she thought I understood her. By repeating these things back to her, it allowed her to feel heard and understood.

I then suggested several industry positions that would be available to her if the companies had training programs. All the positions would be able to utilize her degree of study and allow her to engage her passions.

Purpose is an important element in determining your candidate's quest for success. If you can determine their true purpose, passion, and skills, and seek a training program that will allow them to transfer into an available job, it's a win-win for all. The new method works. We all must take the time to ask the right questions and find solutions to our upcoming talent shortage. The people are out there; we have just been looking in the wrong places.

CHAPTER 5

FOR THE JOB SEEKER

The Search for Alignment

We all come to crossroads in our lives. Applicants often come to me thinking that if they only had the perfect job, everything in their life would be wonderful. I've interviewed many different types of people over the years and have noticed that the real issue is often not simply the quest for the right job but the quest to find their real purpose in life. And finding one's purpose is an answer that always comes from the inside out, not from the outside in.

No exterior force, whether it be a job, a relationship, or even winning lottery numbers, is going to provide everlasting happiness for every individual. Being out of alignment with who you are—the core of your person—allows you to make decisions based on factors that don't resonate with your own personal uniqueness. We are all different, but I've outlined some common strategies that can assist you in reaching your own unique goal of happiness. If you are at your own personal crossroads, the five steps in The Faremouth Method will help you take stock and choose your next direction with vision and purpose.

Sometimes a predictive test can also be helpful. There are many tools available these days that can uncover the untapped potential within you. If you feel your life isn't what you want it to be, dig deeper. The answers can be found. And I know some of you have to work a job right now just to handle your financial situations, but there are still ways to move your life toward your true purpose. Sometimes, it all starts with getting involved in a hobby or activity that brings you joy. Don't settle for just an ordinary life. Make it a spectacular life. Aligning yourself with the passions and talents that are yours, and yours alone, is what you, as a person, are here to do.

Happiness can't be found by looking for exterior solutions. It has to come from within you.

Maybe a little self-inventory can help you access your gifts. What have you done in your life that gives you joy? What achievements and accomplishments have you experienced that made you truly happy? As a recruiter and placement counselor for the last thirty years, I've asked my applicants questions like these, which have helped me help them get in touch with their gifts.

Start by Taking a Break

Sometimes in life, we have tools available to us that could help us get to our destination, but we don't recognize them or choose not to take advantage of them. We all have a particular destination toward which we want to go. But we may have times in our life where we need to step away from the wheel, get off the path, and take a break. When we are in the day-to-day trenches of life, we can become weary, tired, and overwhelmed. Sometimes, to arrive at the right destination, we need to get off the road for a bit and recharge.

Finding a job, or changing your career path, can be a perilous journey. With so many choices available, which one do we choose? Which path do we take? How do we get there successfully? I think there is a real advantage to taking time off to recharge. All cell phones, computers, and technological devices need to be recharged. If we use a technological device and never charge the battery, what happens to it? It dies, doesn't it? It quits running. So, shouldn't it be the same for human beings?

I came upon an article recently that suggested people try to take a vacation before they start a new job, and I agree. We can take all the assessment tests in the world, see every recruiter in town, interview all kinds of places, but if our minds are tired and weary, we might make the wrong decision and take the wrong path. And you don't need to go somewhere else to recharge. You can simply do things like yoga or meditation or just sit in your backyard and read a good book. Or go out with a trusted friend and have fun. The important thing is getting the downtime you need to recharge.

If you have been searching for your new destination, career path, or job, maybe what you need to do at this very moment is stop. Stop and take a break. Find out what you can do to step back, rest, and clear your head before you continue down your current path. The right job for you is out there, but taking a break can ensure that you are healthy enough to recognize it when it appears.

At the Crossroads

Most of us, at some point in our lives, have to find a job. It's rare that a person is born knowing what they want to do, grows up and gets the proper training or degree, works in a job for most of their adult life, and lives happily ever after. It usually doesn't work that way. For many of us, we are born into a family, are influenced by our parents and their achievements, or lack thereof, find a subject or course of study that interests us, seek training or formal education to develop our skill interest, graduate or not, and have to seek employment to be able to pay our bills.

But what if you find yourself at a major crossroads in your life? For whatever reason, be it personal or business, you are without a job and all the traditional methods of finding the right job are not available to you. Or they may be available and the job offers are just not coming in?

I always choose to see my cup as half full. Like everyone, I've had my share of losses, failures, disappointment, and tragedy. But for me, those great losses forced me to look inside myself, see what I'm made of as a person, and gain the inner strength to go to a better place.

If you are standing at a crossroads in your life, or in a job that you hate going into every single day, you do have choices. And the choices you make are critical to your future empowerment.

Five Steps of The Faremouth Method
for the Job Seeker

Step 1. Do a Self-Inventory

Looking for a job, or having just lost one, forces you to stop, reevaluate, and try to move to a better place. Forget what's on your resume for a minute. What are your most important assets, beliefs, values, and passions? What gives you joy? What skills or interests do you bring to the table? What are your greatest accomplishments? In what type of business office or corporate structure do you do your best work? If you could magically have any job, what job would you choose and why would you choose it?

Be honest with yourself when doing this inventory!

Calm down, and begin to take a good hard look at who you are and what your interests and past achievements might be. Look at yourself through new eyes and assess some important variables. If you need a place to start, ask yourself some of the following self-evaluation questions:

As a child, what experiences gave you the most fulfillment?

Review your childhood experiences and see where they take you. Go back to the activities you enjoyed most in school. Did you like being president of Junior Achievement? Did you enjoy the debate club? Did you really have fun in art class? Sometimes, the early experiences that gave you joy can help you on your journey to discovering a whole new career path.

What are your strong beliefs and core values?

This is a tough one. Early childhood beliefs and conditioning can throw us totally off course. Start by making a list of beliefs and values you hold dear. No one has to see the list, so put it all down. This is your life, and you need to outline what you truly think and feel. For those who feel blocked, career counselor Roy Cohen encourages his clients "to try an activity that neutralizes and contains the distractions, such as meditation, yoga, or a [. . .] wilderness immersion program [. . .]. 'Sometimes people are in such a familiar place that they can't think creatively,' Cohen explains. 'They need to remove themselves as much as possible from their comfort zone, so that the roles they typically play are stripped away. Being on their own and relying on their initiative to survive and thrive is often transformative. It may take six months of meditating plus a wilderness trip plus therapy, but collectively those experiences will produce a spark and something will emerge from the process'" (quoted in Wood 2014).

Who do you look up to and admire, and why?

The person doesn't have to be Steve Jobs or Bill Gates. They are great contributors to our global society, but you don't have to have icons so grandiose. It might be a favorite teacher or coach. A candidate named Mark admired his high school baseball coach. He told me, when I interviewed him, that his coach was brilliant at team-building and working with every player's strengths and weaknesses. He said he made it fun to be a part of the team. He cared about his players and did all he could to bring out the best in them. That struck a chord with Mark, and he greatly admired those traits in his coach. Mark went on to say that, after every game, the coach got all the parents together and highlighted every single player. He also told me with a big smile that he remembered the coach saying about one of his weakest players, "He almost caught that fly ball!" He cared about people, and that was important to Mark. Mark said he learned a lot from his coach about how to deal with people. Having good people skills was one of Mark's best assets. I placed Mark in a sales trainee position for an oilfield service company. He's gone on to produce record-breaking profits for his company and has quickly moved up the ladder. Being able to deal with people in a job was important to Mark. He needed a career that utilized those core values and beliefs. A sales career aligned beautifully to who he was.

What global causes do you hold near and dear to your heart?

How could you use your professional or education credentials to help those causes? Check out Yahoo headlines, watch the evening news, or read the paper. What's going on in the world that gets your attention? Many people feel they want to totally get out of the field they are in. What if your skill set could be utilized in a manner to help those causes? It might bring you fulfillment without having to totally change direction. One candidate, Sam, had a degree in journalism. He worked as a technical writer for a seismic company. He found the work boring and grinding. He had absolutely no passion for what he was doing. He loved watching the news and loved watching the reporters out in the field. He was placed with a large manufacturing company that dealt with risk processes. He's excited about his new career and enjoys working in the field and dealing with disasters.

What accomplishments have you made that you are most proud?

Another candidate, Sally, focused on her accomplishments and found a successful career because of it. She came to me as a chemical engineer with a major chemical manufacturer, and she was miserable. The company she worked for had a sterile feel to it; she had to wear lab coats and felt so regimented that she wanted totally out of the field. The creative element was nowhere to be found. When I asked her about her accomplishments, she told me about a hobby she had utilizing her artistic talents. She made special, aromatic soaps from the ingredients produced on her family's dairy farm. Sally started going to craft fairs and selling more product than any other booth. She so enjoyed her hobby, and one day she even met a famous person who owned a chain of specialty shops. She began selling her soaps at this famous chain of stores and now does over $1 million in sales annually.

Sally took her accomplishments with her chemistry background and reinvented her career. She stayed true to her core, which was indicative of a creative, artistic person who understood the makeup of various chemical processes. She took her passion, dedication, and hard work and changed her career direction. She now couldn't be happier. She stayed true to her core and who she was without having to start all over again and go back to school to totally change direction.

What goals have you set for yourself?

Sometimes this step can be easier with the help of a skilled professional, such as a career coach, counselor, therapist, or mentor. Cohen states, "Since successful people tend to be metrics- and model-driven, they need to begin with research and information gathering, assess and evaluate what they have learned, and then turn that insight into a life plan that is more meaningful" (quoted in Wood 2014). This is a big step; if you don't have support and guidance, it might seem too difficult to do alone. Accomplishing it, however, can crystalize your path and provide helpful information on what you need to do to get there.

Write your obituary.

I know this sounds morbid. But ask yourself how you want to be remembered by those around you and how you might be able to make a greater contribution to the world. We all have limited time on this earth. The years seem to go by faster and faster. According to William Winn, a psychologist with the advisory firm New Directions, "your 30s, 40s and 50s are an intense time at work and in building relationships, and the self takes a backseat to all of this." But to find your true passions, you need to slow down, "press the reset button and ask, *What matters to ME now?*" (quoted in Wood 2014). Writing your obituary might be the necessary exercise to find the answer to such a question. What do you want people to say about you? Wouldn't it be sad if all they said was "They were a great person. They had so much potential; too bad they didn't have more time on this earth to actualize it"?

A self-inventory might provide you with keen insight that allows you to actualize your gifts for the next, more fulfilling stage of your life.

Step 2. Ask Better Questions

As a job seeker, you will hopefully ask skillful questions at every stage of finding a recruiter and meeting prospective employers.

Skillful and well-thought-out questions put to you by interviewers can help evaluate skills and passions, not just degrees and years of experience. Quality questions create a quality life. And isn't a better quality of life what we are all seeking? But we must take the time to ask different questions. For example, ask yourself the following important questions: What are your true interests? What position might be available based on your traits, passions, interests, skills, and abilities? Could you seek out a skilled professional to assist you with your search? Are you up for relocation? Do you have a workable resume and is your profile updated on LinkedIn? What networking groups could you join to broaden your search? Could you make your job search a full-time job? How could you make contacts with colleagues, supervisors, or even competitors and inform them of your current availability? Asking and answering these questions will get you focused on your goals and the steps it takes to reach them.

Step 3. Step Out of Your Comfort Zone

"Life begins at the end of our comfort zone." And for job seekers, this is true in the current market now more than ever. Instead of only applying to directly related companies and their openings, reach out to other areas and industries that may have current openings your skill set could translate into. For example, if you have a degree in mechanical engineering and have worked with pumps, could your skills transfer into a mechanical engineering position that works with compressors, water treatment plants, etc.?

If you shy away from new areas due to fear of failure, consider making baby steps toward expanding your career horizons. Take classes, manage new projects in your current job, and volunteer in a field that interests you; all of these can empower you toward a significant career move.

Step 4. Take Your Time and Do It Right

At every stage of job seeking, an applicant must take the time to make strong and careful decisions. Needing a job and being without one for an extended time are factors that can speed up the job search process. But remember to make one decision at a time; speed often leads to costly mistakes in the quest to find the right job. Do your homework, and be strategic. Make yourself a plan for the day, week, or month, and then work your plan.

Do not apply for the same type of job merely because it's all you think you can do. Instead, utilize every resource available to you to ensure that you pursue a career that aligns with your personality and goals. For example, take assessment tests to track your interests or passions, research careers that fit with your personality, and observe professionals in the fields you're considering. You can even visit a professional career counselor to help you find a more fulfilling career. Or you can seek a new career from the comfort of your phone. With the ever-increasing growth of technology, mobile job-search apps have become widely used among job seekers. Such apps give "users the accessibility to keep up with the latest job openings, and the privacy to pursue new opportunities on their own mobile device" (Beyond 2011). Such apps include LinkedIn and Indeed.

Step 5. Be a hunter

Finally, be a hunter. If you want to keep your job, take on more responsibility at work. The days of "that is not in my job description" are long gone. If you are searching for a job, strive to exceed a potential employer's expectations. If you desire a job in a new field or with a different company, you must invest all your mental resources into *hunting* for the information necessary to attain your new job. If you want to excel in this market, you cannot just take *some* initiative. You must take *more* initiative than your competitors, fiercely seeking opportunity in the manner of a hungry wolf. If you do this, you will surpass the many "gatherers" who expect opportunities to fall into their laps.

You must be extremely proactive and chase after what you want. Just like a fisherman determined to get the perfect catch, if the fish are not in your area, you need to keep moving the boat; you don't stay in one place for days on end. You go to a different spot, embrace a different opportunity, and *make* things happen instead of just *waiting* for them to.

If you have the passion and your skills do align with the job, there is light at the end of the tunnel. But don't take the easy way out. True success just might be preparation meeting opportunity. In this tough market, if you want to land your dream job, do your homework and work hard to get what you want. Going the extra mile usually does pay off. This alternative method of hiring can work. All your efforts and hard work will pay off if you have the passion, skills, and desire to do it. Find out what gives you joy in a job and go for it. Sitting back and waiting for opportunities to come to you isn't going to cut the mustard in most cases. Don't expect the easy way out. It usually doesn't let you achieve your important goals. Be willing to go the extra mile; when you are willing to do the extra work, amazing things can happen. I know they can. I see it every single day, and I'm proud to represent those outstanding candidates who do what it takes to get where they want to go. Are you one of those candidates? Only you can decide what's best for you. The ball is in your court. Do what it takes, and you will be happy you did.

Eleven Ways to Know If You Are in the Wrong Job

How do you know when you are in the wrong job? Are you chronically late for work, take extra time at lunch, leave ten minutes before five? Maybe you really don't want to be there. Maybe the job you are in isn't properly aligned with your passions and commitments. Are you doing what you want to do or what you were told you should be doing? Keep these thoughts in mind to determine if you need to change your direction and find a more fulfilling job:

I. *Your input is not taken seriously.*
    We all have something to offer. Whether we have a degree from an Ivy League school or a high school diploma, we all have valuable contributions to make. Throughout my years of placing high-potential candidates, I have learned that a degree is no guarantee that you will be successful. Look at Bill Gates, Steve

Jobs, and countless other extremely successful people who have taken innovative ideas and made revolutionary changes, making a significant impact on the world. When your boss or company shoots down your ideas, or even laughs at your suggestions, it's not only insulting, it's demotivating. Pretty soon, you stop caring.

2. *You never hear the word* Thanks.
   We all need to feel appreciated. It's a basic human need. We all need to know we do something well. And everyone, even poor performers, do some things well. If you are constantly being criticized for your performance, eventually you start believing you are unworthy and begin to take the feelings of unworthiness home with you. They can rub off on family and friends and lead to unhealthy relationships in every part of your life. Life is too short to walk around feeling like you are "less than" and everyone around you is more worthy of happiness.

3. *Your boss is the top dog.*
   If you feel that your performance is only serving the greater glory and advancement of your boss, it may be time to move on. Life is too short to spend your time developing your boss's career at the expense of your own. A great boss knows that if their team succeeds, and each of the people on that team succeeds, then they succeed too.

4. *The criticism you receive is made in public.*
   Constructive feedback can be a huge motivator. We all need a little nudge. We all need to be told how we can do something better. But it's the delivery of the message and where it's done that is key here. Such things need to be discussed in private. If you are repeatedly told you are an idiot and your ideas are worthless, or you are always criticized in public, it greatly affects your self-esteem. Life's too short to be humiliated constantly. It's demotivating and takes the wind out of your sails. Get off this road, and get to an environment where you are not constantly attacked.

5. *You feel like you have no purpose.*
   Everyone likes to feel like they are part of a master plan. We were all put on this earth with special gifts and talents. Everyone likes to feel they make an impact—not just on paper results but on the lives of other people. Life's too short to go home every day feeling like you have worked without accomplishing anything meaningful. If your boss doesn't stop to ask you about your family, to discuss informally whether you need any help, or even to just say a kind word, then you are only a cog in a larger machine.

6. *You are treated like a number.*
   We are all replaceable; everyone works for a payday. But most people want to work for more than just a paycheck. You want to work for people you respect and admire, and you want to be respected and admired in return. You also want to work for people who can elevate you to a higher level. Staying stuck in a meaningless job with no rewards in sight is not a good place to be. Move on. There are other situations that can bring you greater fulfillment.

7. *You are not excited to go to work.*
   There are no jobs where every day is wonderful. But if there are too many days you dread going to your job, then the writing is on the wall. Every job should have more fun days than dreary ones. Life's too short to go in every single day and only wait for five o'clock to arrive.

8. *You can't see a fulfilling future.*
   Every job should lead to something—hopefully a promotion. Abraham Maslow discusses this in his hierarchy of needs (quoted in McLeod 2007). We as human beings need to know there will be some type of advancement. Maybe that's only a new, more exciting project. But feeling stuck in a job that's going nowhere can be demotivating and lead to sadness and depression.

9. *You don't think you have the skill set to do anything else.*
   If you feel like you are incapable of doing anything but your

current job, that's the best reason to quit it, because you will quickly find that it isn't true. Of course, you shouldn't quit unless you have other options on the horizon. It's always better to leave for a new opportunity when you already have one. You may feel like you have too much time invested with the company, your family will be in jeopardy, or you can't find a job in a location close to where you live. All those things are true only if you let them be true. Take risks, believe you have a meaningful contribution to make in this world, and trust that there is a new opportunity that can align with your special skills and abilities.

10. *You feel like the victim, not the victor.*

You do have choices in this life. It's up to you whether you will consider yourself a victor or a victim. Change is necessary for growth. Believe you can do great things, and you will. You have the power to go through this life with much happiness, fulfillment, and success. Become the victor and make the choices that will align with the victor within you.

11. *You can't be you.*

If your job is in total misalignment with who you are, it's time to consider moving on. While in college, I worked as an analyst. I had to work with numbers, charts, chemical results from a lab, etc. I had little contact with people, and I was miserable. As soon as I received my degree, I started my new job search. The job was a good experience because it taught me how to place analytical people. But it was the absolute worse job match for me.

Your Integrity Is in Every Move

Personal integrity is an important pattern of behavior that goes with you your entire life. Thinking you are going to outsmart a recruiter, job application, or prospective employer usually ends up blowing up in your face. Trying to portray yourself as someone or something you are not is a dangerous exercise that gets you nowhere. Essentially, not being honest is just one big roadblock to your progress. In my career, I've seen a lot of misrepresentations of education, degrees, actual work experience, etc., and at the end of the day it's one big recipe for disaster. We are all human. We all make mistakes. We all take wrong turns in our lives. It's part of life. It just happens. But it's not what happens to us that really matters anyway. It's how we handle it. And more importantly, what are the lessons we learn from the mistakes we make.

And being dishonest or not having integrity gets messy. It reminds me of the Enron situation, where not being honest and having no integrity caused the demise of a wonderful company, and the effects of many people losing stock options, pensions, and jobs had far-reaching ramifications. It was ugly, painful, and flat out disastrous for many. And it all started with someone thinking it was okay to be dishonest. It isn't. Fudging your resume or twisting the facts, thinking you will gain more by doing this, just won't work. Below is a list of things to avoid when trying to find your dream job.

What *Not to Do* as an Applicant When Looking for a Job

1. *Don't have a substandard resume.*

   If you can't put together a good resume on your own, then you can pay a professional to do it. But make sure when they do the resume for you, they retain *your* voice and style. If they write in a way wholly different from you and how you naturally communicate, then a recruiter and employer will find your resume inauthentic and you will seem less than authentic.

2. *Don't list a degree under Education on your resume if you don't have one.*

   If you are in the process of getting a degree and it's May but your graduation date is the following December, put *Expected graduation date:* and then the appropriate month and year. If you have enough credits to have a degree but never did the paperwork or got the actual degree, don't put a degree on the resume. Make sure your situation is clear on the resume. If an employer calls the registrar and is told you don't have a degree when you say you do, the chances of being considered for a job become slim to none. It speaks of a lack of integrity.

3. *Don't leave big gaps on your resume.*
   If you have been a dog walker for the last six years because your mom has had cancer and she was all alone and depended on you to care for her, don't leave it off the resume or call yourself something misrepresentative of what you did. For example, don't call yourself something like *wildlife manager* or *behavioral supervisor*. Give yourself a generic title, list your degrees or education at the top of the resume, and present an honest picture of employment. Establish as many correlations as you can of skills that may transfer into other areas, but make sure you don't do any actual misrepresentation on the resume.

4. *Don't fabricate references or list people who had nothing to do with your previous jobs.*
   It amazes me how small even the largest city actually is. In my hometown of Houston, people know people, and if you fabricate a reference and it's discovered that they weren't, in fact, a previous employer of yours, it can cost you a job offer or have you terminated if you've already gotten the job before the information is discovered.

5. *Don't be careless when listing information for a criminal background check.*
   Seek the advice of an attorney on how to present this information. This is a delicate area, and you need professional advice from the legal community to know how to handle it correctly on a resume and in an interview.

6. *Don't list skills that you don't have on your resume.*
   If you were in a call center and your job was to answer incoming calls, don't list that you were an inside sales representative that handled logistics. If you misrepresent what you did and are hired to do something you have never done, your new boss will not be happy that you misrepresented your skill set and will have a lack of trust in you from the get go.

   Being honest is important. Skills can be learned on a job, but once trust is broken, it's hard to repair it and be considered a person of integrity. Your reputation also follows you your entire career. Make sure you present yourself in the best way possible, having honesty and integrity high on your list of skills to bring to the table. You will never go wrong with this practice. Never.

Three Steps for Negotiating the Best Offer

We all want to be compensated well for our worth. In today's job market, getting the best offer can be considered an art. There are proven methods, however, that can benefit you in this negotiating process.

In my years as an executive recruiter, I have instructed many applicants to interview in such a way that lands them a good offer. But as I have mentioned, interviewing is an art, and it doesn't matter what you've accomplished in your career; if you aren't thinking about the negotiating process before you even interview, you've already put yourself in a compromised position.

The following tips can assist you with this process. I have worked with all kinds of applicants through the years, and I know these strategies work and produce satisfying offers.

What You Have to Be

You must be prepared. Before you are scheduled to interview with the company, you must do your homework. You have to take the time to know everything you can about the company and how your background contributes to the bottom line. Don't think that, just because you have the right degree, the right GPA, and the right tenure, you will land a whopper of an offer. It just won't happen. You have to know everything and more about the company and demonstrate how your background is a good match for the job.

I recently had a candidate, who we will call Brian, who landed a wonderful offer. Brian did not have the exact background for the job he was interviewing for, but he had the transferrable skills that allowed him to make a valuable contribution and land an outstanding offer. He went onto the company website and researched extensively. He knew who their clients were, what their revenues had been for the last several years, and what the company's goals and corporate strategies were. He also knew they were in a period of transition as the current VP was retiring. He knew their website was outdated and needed a total facelift to present this company in a more updated manner to prospective customers. He knew that in his years as a sales manager, he had taken companies to amazing results and increased revenues significantly. And while his background was not one in which he worked directly with the industry, he had sold to the same end-users and had the relationships and contacts that would benefit the company expeditiously. He made a list of the contacts he had, showed the sales revenues he had increased, and demonstrated what he did in his previous jobs to motivate a sales staff to produce more. All these achievements that he listed in his preparation mode translated, in the eyes of the client, into increased revenues and growth for the company. His salary requirements were a drop in the bucket compared to the increase in revenue his contributions would make to quickly expand the company and affect the bottom line.

Brian's strong research and preparation for this interview started the negotiating process well before he ever got in front of the client. Because he took the time to understand the company and their goals, he was able to present information that demonstrated his competency and how he would stand heads above other, more experienced candidates. He also took the time, through his networking and extensive research, to know that the president had a role outside of the office that he had once had himself. The president had been a minister in his church, and Brian had had the same role at one point in his life. Working side by side with someone of similar interests was something that could greatly enhance his chances of landing a good offer. "Birds of a feather flock together," as the saying goes. And people like to work with similar types of people. They relate to those individuals better. So Brian took the time to find this out about this executive, and it impressed his interviewer greatly.

What You Have to Do

You have to do more than necessary. When the day came for the interview, Brian did all the right things to come across as impressive. He arrived at the interview thirty minutes early, which demonstrated his excitement and interest in conducting this interview. He took a trial run to the interviewing location the night before to make sure he would arrive at the correct place and avoid traffic problems. He also contacted people whom the president knew from professional affiliations and asked them to write letters about his performance that they had supervised through the years, and he took the letters with him. He specifically asked them to outline in the reference letters accomplishments he had made that related directly to what was important to their companies at the period of their growth.

Having others validate our worth on paper can be a powerful tool in negotiations. Having someone a prospective interviewer respects put their stamp of approval on you can often be more effective in validating your achievements than you can on your own. All these steps translate into increasing your worth to a company, which makes your salary requirements reasonable and worthwhile.

Brian also took the time before the second interview to put a marketing plan together to illustrate what he would do in the first thirty, sixty, and ninety days. He called it an action plan. He also researched projects he knew were on the horizon that would need the company's products—new projects the company had not been involved with in the past. That would translate into increased revenues for the company and expansive growth strategies. This gained the president's attention; to him, all of Brian's efforts translated into an employee who would go the extra mile.

What You Can Have

To earn a great offer and negotiate the salary we desire, we have to take steps necessary to put ourselves in a position of worth. Keep these tips in mind when you negotiate for the best offer. It will provide you with the necessary ingredients to make your worth obvious to a client. Not taking the time to do what is necessary *before* the interview will land you only a mediocre offer. Negotiating and interviewing in the correct manner is crucial to landing you the job of your dreams.

Assessment Tests

There are times in life you might feel stuck. As an applicant, you might not understand what your true skills are or what careers would utilize those strengths. You might feel frustrated, disappointed, and unhappy with the choices you have made and are not sure how to turn your situation around. The following assessment tests have proven helpful to job seekers in making a more complete inventory of their skills and have provided them with insights that have allowed them to make better choices toward securing long-term careers that fit them. A skillful employment recruiter can assist with this process, but if that is not an option you choose to take, the following assessment tests may be very helpful.

There is a famous Greek inscription at the Temple of Apollo in Delphi that translates to *know thyself*. There have been many books and articles written about this famous inscription throughout the years. It sounds like a basic premise, but oftentimes, because of many complicated life conditions, we find ourselves at odds with such a sentiment. We could have had adverse conditioning in our childhood that prevents us from coming to terms with knowing our true selves. Or we could be trying to live up to another person's idea of who we are and what we should do on our life path.

The following assessment tools will hopefully allow those lost on their career path to find more clarity and helpful information. However, this list is not all-inclusive. Just like with cell phones and other technology, improvements are always being made, and other tools may be available to you. And no one test is best for everyone. We are all different, with different aptitudes and abilities. You might need to use more than one of these, or find a different one altogether, to get the information you need.

Six Assessment Tools Available to Candidates:

1. *Myers-Briggs (www.myersbriggs.org)*

   The Myers-Briggs Type Indicator (MBTI) personality inventory brings the theory of psychological types, as described by C. G. Jung, to people in a way that is understandable and useful. The theory essentially states that much of the seemingly random variation in people's behavior is actually quite orderly and consistent due to the basic differences between various individuals' preferred use of their perceptions and judgment. "Perception involves all the ways of becoming aware of things, people, happenings, or ideas. Judgment involves all the ways of coming to conclusions about what has been perceived. If people differ systematically in what they perceive and in how they reach conclusions, then it is only reasonable for them to differ correspondingly in their interests, reactions, values, motivations, and skills.' C. G. Jung" ("MBTI Basics" 2017). The best reason to choose the MBTI instrument to discover your personality type is the hundreds of studies completed over the past forty years that have proven it to be both valid and reliable. In other words, it measures what it says it does (validity) and produces the same results when given more than once (reliability). The MBTI instrument uses eight preferences to make up your personality type. Each personality type comes with different interests and views that can help you in determining your career path.

2. *Birkman (www.birkman.com)*

   The Birkman Method is an assessment with 250 true/false and 48 multiple-choice questions. Although it is long, it provides quick feedback directly after the test is completed. This test is utilized to help determine your strengths, expectations, stress behaviors, and motivations, which can lead you to being successful. It will help predict behavior and work satisfaction in many different situations. It helps improve people skills and puts together roles and relationships for higher productivity and success.

3. *The Princeton Review (www.princetonreview.com)*
   The Princeton Review provides a list of careers and thorough descriptions, including requirements for obtaining each career choice. There is also a section on how to achieve your dream career.

4. *The Balance (www.thebalance.com/different-types-of-jobs-a-z-list-2059643)*
   The Balance website provides many valuable resources to assist the job search process. The listed link provides a list of links, each of which provides requirements for a different job title within a listed field.

5. *Kolbe (www.kolbe.com)*
   The Kolbe assessments identify people's natural instincts, also known as cognitive skills. The theory behind it states that creative instincts are the source of the mental energy that drive people to take specific actions. These tests will help determine a person's modus operandi (MO), which governs actions, reactions, and interactions, and helps with a person's use of time and natural form of communication. When you can control the creative instincts, you will have the freedom to be your own self. When you compare a person's MO to the given task, you can see how closely their personality will align with self-expectation and the requirements for the task. This test is effective because it focuses on the cognitive part of the mind, which includes a person's drive, necessity, innate force, instinct, mental energy, and talents.

6. *The MAPP Career Test (www.assessment.com)*
   The MAPP test is a fifteen-minute assessment with seventy-one different traits and three different statements. It lists a series of statements, which you would put in order from most preferred to least preferred. Once you get the results, you are scored against nine hundred jobs and presented with those that would fit you best. The site also shows you what education you might need, as well as real job openings in your area.

Making the Most of an Interview

The following are a few important tips for preparing for and performing in an interview. They could be a saving grace in helping you both land the job you want and negotiate the salary you desire:

1. Do a thorough investigation of the company and its history.

2. Know how your skills and experience can contribute to the company.

3. Understand the job description, and present how your skills, attitude, and experience are a good fit.

4. Always ask questions at the end of the interview, such as:

    - What qualities do the top performers at your company possess that have made them stand out?
    - What would you expect me to achieve in my first thirty, sixty, and ninety days?
    - What areas of this job do you consider most important?
    - What type of additional training could I seek to get up to speed in a timely manner?

Make Sure Your Recruiter Is Helping You

When you have lost a job, or have decided to find a better one, it's important to find a recruiter who you feel has your best interests at heart. The following are some considerations to keep in mind when you are on the hunt for a recruiting professional who can assist you:

1. Is the recruiter experienced in your area of interest? If not, do they have the resources to refer you to others who might be more helpful?

2. Is the recruiter taking the time to hear you? Do they not just look at the resume but listen to what you really enjoy? For example, if you have a degree in finance but have decided that

you don't want to work in accounting with just numbers and spreadsheets and that you enjoy IT or computers, are they suggesting careers where your skills will transfer? Do they offer resources for you to get the training you might need to make such a career transition? If they try to convince you to only pursue finance-related jobs after you have told them how you don't want to do so any longer, are they really trying to assist you in what might be best *for you*?

3. If you want references on them, are they willing to provide them?

4. How do they represent their brand? Are there helpful tips on their website that give you solid advice?

5. If you have been on several interviews but not gotten any offers, are they investigating with you what you might be doing wrong? Are they doing mock interviews with you before you go on future interviews to help you present yourself and your background in a way that is more advantageous to you?

Five Steps to Help You Find Your True Passion

We've all heard it before: "Do what you love," or "Follow your passion." Yet passion in your work life is a concept that is difficult to explain, hard to find, and impossible to measure. It is a quality that is unique to each of us and has no one sure way to find it. In a world that quickly evolves and changes, a college degree is no longer a guarantee for finding a job, and a job no longer provides stability. So if we are currently living in a world where change is more of a constant than stability is, how do we embrace our passion and get direction to better understand what we are looking for.

Passion can be described as something that lights us up and gives us tremendous joy, a yearning of some type that gives us much personal, as well as professional, fulfillment. Some people refer to passion as one's *calling*. It might be something you are born knowing, but for many it is something that must be discovered over time. We all know the person who wanted to be a doctor or lawyer in grade school, took that path, and lived happily ever after. They were fortunate enough to discover their calling at a young age and carry it with them going forward. For most of us, such an understanding is discovered throughout our life.

What you are passionate about largely depends on what point you are at in life. Breathe easy; rest assured that there is more than one dream job out there for each of us! Growing up, I wanted to be a lawyer. My dad (who was from Europe) told me that such a career would not be good for me as many of the lawyers he knew were "different" and I would have a hard time competing in such a tough arena. At the time, I thought my father was so wise, and I chose another career path that I thought was better for me.

If you have not found your calling yet, don't worry. When you do discover it, it will come at the right time. Never wish that you had uncovered it sooner. Your desires today are not what you would have wanted ten years ago. The knowledge you have acquired over time is what will enable you to recognize the right opportunity when it comes your way.

However, just because you haven't found your calling yet, doesn't mean you can't seek it out. The following steps can help you in the right direction toward discovering your true passion:

1. *Make Your Current Job a Learning Ground*
    Embrace this time of employment to advance your skills. Study what you are being asked to do, try new things, and attack any fears you have. If you are in sales, try new marketing methods; if you're a project manager, ask to be put on different types of projects to expand your experience. You have nothing to lose, but you could gain a lot in preparation for your next role.

2. *Understand Why You Might Be Unhappy in Your Current Job*
    It is important to understand what you don't like about your current job, so you can make appropriate changes in your next role. Once you have pinpointed the sources of pain, consider whether they have been issues in past positions. Ask yourself if you might be in the right job but have the wrong boss? A wrong

boss can totally warp your perception of the right job. If it's a wrong boss, maybe a good talk would solve the problem. If they're not open to discussion, maybe a similar company and position would be the solution.

3. *Do Your Homework*
   What you learn from your self-analysis will determine which direction to go in next. Discovering your passion may take some trial and error, but it all starts with a high level of homework, or research. If you are planning to change industries, begin to explore different sectors. If something piques your interest, see if it resonates with your core values and who you are.

4. *Apply Yourself*
   When you find a path you want to pursue, kick your studying of that field into overdrive. Attend as many face-to-face events with people in the field as you possibly can, connect with contacts in the field, find ways to volunteer in the new area, ask a lot of questions, and take advantage of time you have available outside of your current job to fully apply yourself to learning all you can.

5. *Provide Value and Master the Skill*
   You need to demonstrate that you have valuable assets to offer. You need to differentiate yourself from the competition by illustrating to a prospective employer the value you can bring to their company. It is only then that you will have a real advantage and be attractive to a new employer. Explaining how you have mastered the skill set they are needing and giving examples of how you can affect their bottom line will give you a much better chance at being hired. Telling a prospective employer how great you are is one thing. Telling them *why* you are great for their company with concrete examples is a much better game plan that will give you a strong advantage toward getting hired.

The $9 Million Baseball Player

I had an applicant once by the name of Robert. Robert was a special young man. He came to see me after moving back to Houston from Dallas after losing his job. I asked Robert what he had experienced in his life that made him truly happy. He told me he had been the captain of his baseball team in high school and took them to a national competition and won. He told me he tutored students in math and enjoyed seeing them do well on tests after he helped them with their struggles with learning. He said he had been given a baseball scholarship to a major university, but he hadn't gone because his dad had died suddenly and Robert had had some tough emotional challenges to overcome. After his dad died, he moved to Dallas to get away from all the familiar people and places. While in Dallas, he took a job as a waiter at a famous diner. He said he made more tips than any other waiter there. One time, a famous major league team owner came in and left him a five-hundred-dollar tip.

Well, I thought to myself, this tells me a whole lot about this young man. He is a team player, he's competitive, he's service-oriented, and he's good with numbers. Maybe a sales job selling a technical product would align him with his own unique gifts and talents. I picked up the phone and called the president of a company I was working with at the time. I told them Robert's story, and reluctantly they agreed to see him. They interviewed Robert and hired him on a temporary basis. Well, the rest is history. Robert sold $9 million worth of pipe in the first year. He received a $55K bonus the second Christmas he was there, because the second year he sold $15 million worth of pipe. Robert is now the lead sales representative for the company.

Robert was able to align his passions and gifts to the right job. And Robert drives thirty miles each day to work. But he's happy to do this because he's so happy when he gets to work. I saw Robert not long ago, and his smile stretched from ear to ear. He told me he's engaged to be married and couldn't be happier. He told me he also felt he might become a partner of the firm someday because he was so valuable to their success. And maybe it's not a job that will do this for you. Maybe you want to be a supermom, work with the PTA, and help in the lunchroom. Maybe the job of being a nurturing mother can make you shine. Or maybe you enjoyed art in high school and want to become an artist. Getting in touch with your inner light can make all the difference between just a good life and a great life. We all have our special gifts and talents. Don't give up finding out what your talents might be. You can do this.

The Power of Focus

Doesn't it feel good when you do something you enjoy and achieve a goal? I remember the smile on my young son's face when he broke a brick in Tae Kwon Do for the first time. He was grinning from ear to ear. He had always been a shy child; he didn't talk until he was four years old, and he always hid behind my legs when he met new people. At the age of four, we enrolled him in a Tae Kwon Do class, and to this day I truly believe it helped his ability to focus tremendously.

But what's all this talk we hear about focus? Is there really anything to it? Does being able to focus enable us to achieve more than if we don't? I know it does. And I also think exercises like martial arts, Tai Chi, yoga, etc., can allow us to focus our energy in productive ways that allow us to be more successful. And energy is also something to be considered here. Didn't Einstein say energy cannot be created or destroyed? Well, I'm not going to get into a metaphysical discussion at this time, though that area of study is very interesting to me. But when we focus our energy on what we are passionate about, amazing things can happen. We feel better about ourselves, because accomplishment and success affects our self-esteem; we make valuable contributions to some part of society and we might receive promotions and raises, because we can be more productive and achieve important goals.

If you are struggling with the ability to focus, find help. It will serve you well and amazing results will transpire. Learn to train your mind. Focus, focus, focus. It makes all the difference in how much you can achieve.

Working the Steps of The Faremouth Method When You Have Just Lost Your Job

You wish you could say it was just a bad dream. Your boss called you in today and told you that, despite being a stellar performer and surviving three layoffs, the company has just lost another big contract and they're having a fourth round of layoffs. He's got to let you go.

It's been a great job for over five years, and you've done so well with promotions, achievement awards, and all the good things that go along with success. But the future doesn't look too great, as you are a field engineer in the oil and gas industry and no one is hiring in the industry currently. It's the only job you've had since you graduated college. You were recruited off campus and never had to look for a job. You are scared, upset, and worried.

You were given a small severance package, but it won't last for long. So now what do you do? The first thing you do is *not panic*. And I know it sounds easy for someone else to say, but you can't let panic drive you. You need to take a deep breath, collect your thoughts, and get out a sheet of paper. Be strategic and make a plan. Finding a job is your new full-time job, and with the right determination, planning, networking, and contacts, you will find another job. Consider the following steps—revised for folks who have recently lost their jobs—to put you on the right path:

Step 1. Do a Self-Inventory

This is when you need to get clear on what your skill set is and how it can be transferred into another industry. In this case, if you are an engineer, you need to consider what skills and experiences you have had that would be in demand in the current market. For example, if you worked on a rig and worked with hydraulic equipment, say compressors or pumps, what companies might have products of such a nature with a different industry application? If you have worked in the oilfield, what other industries may use pumps or compressors that could use your expertise in this area? What companies in your current city or state are hiring candidates? Start with local companies, but if relocation is an option, make a list of other companies that may have openings. I always suggest interviewing for more than one opportunity, because it gives a candidate negotiating power. If you have three interviews and you get two offers, you might be able to have the company you prefer match the other offer if you present yourself as a candidate in demand. It doesn't always work out to your advantage, but it often does. Before sending out your resume, make sure it highlights the skills and experiences that relate to each job description. Clearly assess what skills and abilities you have that are in demand in the current market. Do you need to take other courses to make yourself more marketable? For example, if you liked drafting in college but didn't use it much in your last job, could you take a course to make yourself more marketable for current openings? If bills are building up, should you consider taking a night job or part-time job to take some of the pressure off your family for now?

Step 2. Ask Better Questions

You need to ask yourself some serious questions and give yourself honest answers. Consider some of the following: How long can I wait for the perfect job? Can I take a pay cut and prove myself and hopefully be rewarded for my hard work when the market turns around? Can I relocate my family, and if so, where would be the best place to go? What did I like in my previous jobs, and how picky can I get when considering current market conditions? Have I overextended myself? Do we need to sell the house, car, or boat? How can we cut household expenses? Can we reduce cable, eating out, vacations, etc.? Should we have a garage sale? What customers or business contacts do I have who know my work and might have a need for a person with my skill set?

Step 3. Step Out of Your Comfort Zone

If the job you just lost was the only job you have had since college and you never had to interview for jobs much, maybe you need to consider brushing up on your interviewing skills. The following questions may assist you with this process: Should you seek the help of a skilled professional to assist you with the interviewing process?

If you have never had to make cold calls, can you stretch yourself and call companies you're interested in that may not have job openings advertised to see if they might have a need? Can you make a plan to make ten calls daily to prospective companies to inquire about openings? Are you extremely up-to-date on your LinkedIn profile? Does Facebook only portray the most professional information about who you are? Are there networking groups in your industry you could attend to meet people who might know of job leads?

Step 4. Take Your Time and Do It Right

When panic sets in, the worst thing you can do is rush the process and produce a resume with bad spelling or grammatical errors. Make sure your resume is extremely professional. Hire a company to do one if you must. And if your interviewing skills are rusty, polish them up. Many good candidates don't get the jobs because they did not interview correctly. Make a plan for your job search. Work your plan daily. You *must* stay positive. Never mention any negatives on an interview. If you talk negatively about a previous employer, boss, coworker, or industry, it may not serve you in getting the best offer.

Step 5. Be a Hunter

You must be proactive and resourceful. You cannot expect the perfect job to come and find you. Join as many networking groups as you can and seek the assistance of a skilled professional in your industry. Join professional groups and associations—in this case, if you are an engineer, attend the professional engineering seminars and networking groups to hear about what may be going on in your industry. Reach out to your college or university to see if they have a job board or some other career search assistance. Oftentimes, universities work with employers to find candidates from their alumni.

Staying positive, taking care of yourself, and having a strong support group is of the utmost importance during these tough times. You have to believe that you will make it through this hardship and come out stronger, more empowered, and with new relationships and experiences.

Handling Bad News

None of us like bad news. It's painful, disappointing, and stressful. One of the most uncomfortable parts of my job is having to tell an applicant that they didn't get the job. It's a message I don't like to deliver, but it's part of the job and I have to do it. I consider myself a positive person, however, and I always try to see the silver lining in any cloud.

But life is about all kinds of relationships, isn't it? Relationships between men and women, relationships with coworkers and bosses, and most importantly, relationships with ourselves. We all have choices. And at certain times in our lives, for various reasons, we make a choice that comes back to haunt us. At other times, we make better choices that lead us to a happy place. But whatever choice we make in our life, we must deal with the consequences. When we don't get the job we thought was so right for us, we can become angry, frustrated, and defeated. Or we can look within ourselves and try to understand what we may have done that caused the job to not come our way. Or maybe, in some instances, we did everything right, but the job was put on hold or the company had internal goings-on that led them in another direction. The decision to not hire us might have had nothing to do with us at all. But a thorough self-evaluation is still appropriate to try to learn from the experience.

I know, from my many years of doing this job, that a person can have all the qualities necessary—the right degree, experience, and skill set—and the job still might not come their way. I've had many applicants who were so perfect for a job that when the client called and told me they weren't going with that particular candidate, I scratched my head in wonder.

In many cases, I get feedback that the applicant did not interview well. And the longer I do this job, the more I come to understand that interviewing is an art—an art that is very important to master.

One of the suggestions I have made to many applicants through the years is to interview with the mindset of a famous speech made by J. F. Kennedy. He said, "Ask not what your country can do for you;

ask what you can do for your country." Often, I tell applicants to substitute the word *company* for *country*. In other words, I counsel them to tell their prospective employers what *they* as *applicants* can do for the company, rather than ask what the company can do for them. I had one young applicant who went into an interview and, right off the bat, asked the prospective employer how many vacation days he would get, when he would get his first raise, and how soon it would be before he got promoted. Well, suffice to say, it was a short interview. The client was not at all impressed and told me the candidate would not be a fit for the company at all. He saw the candidate as opportunistic and not possessing the true grit necessary to fit with this company. In my long history of doing this job, I know that the candidates who have landed offers have been those who have interviewed in such a way to demonstrate their eagerness to make a contribution to the company. They have outlined how their skills and abilities would enhance the company. They have gone into the interview with a humble attitude and a service orientation. I don't remember ever getting negative feedback from a client about an applicant who handled themselves in such a manner.

And one of the things I always do with candidates is give them honest feedback. It is the only way they can learn and grow and not make the same mistakes again. It's not enjoyable for me to deliver bad news, but I know it's the right thing to do to help the candidate learn from the experience. Telling them what I think they want to hear doesn't help anyone.

Also, even if you don't get the job, you should still write a letter to the company thanking them for their time. People do move around and situations do change. You never know if the job you didn't get may become available again, or if the interviewer or hiring manager might move to another company and need a person with your skill set. Getting upset, angry, or offended because you didn't get the job doesn't serve anyone well—especially yourself. Always hold your head high and handle whatever decision you receive with grace and dignity. It's all about how you handle yourself in any situation. Make sure you always walk away from whatever decision you get with a positive attitude. It will serve you well. If nothing else, it increases your self-confidence and only allows you to grow from the experience. Life is all about choices. Make sure the choices you make in your life are positive, uplifting, and make you feel good about who you are. Blaming others and having a sour, "poor me" pity party is a big waste of time. I know disappointment is not an enjoyable experience, but handling yourself in the proper manner is so important.

The moral of this story? It's not what happens to us in life that really matters. It's how we handle it. Make sure you handle yourself with dignity. It's not easy to do, but it is the right thing to do.

You have to be in touch with your own special gifts and talents to realize what place will take you home to your perfect job. Know what makes your heart sing, and you will be well on your way to finding the answer to your quest. When you align yourself with your passions and desires in the workplace, you will find meaningful employment that will give you the motivation to perform well and achieve much. Be authentic. Do what makes you happy. Don't follow a path that others think is your special destiny. A thorough self-inventory is necessary to arrive at your special place. If you are unsure of what your gifts and talents are, perhaps taking an assessment test can assist you in finding your perfect job or career.

Your Attitude Determines Your Altitude—
Seven Steps to Consider on Layoff Day

If you are lucky enough to not have experienced a layoff, congratulations! But if this situation ever slaps you in the face, your attitude will determine your altitude in where you go from there. Having a positive attitude won't be easy when handling a situation like this. But the way you handle this experience can make all the difference in your professional future.

I. *Don't Flip Out and Show Strong Emotion*
   With any type of loss comes grief and often shock. But you should not show strong emotion when this happens. Keep your

composure, put things in perspective, and don't let the experience break you or damage your self-confidence. You must remember that people from this company might end up working for companies in your future. The way you handle yourself will be remembered. Crying or screaming at your place of work is not a good idea; if you must do either, use the drive home to release these emotions. Your coworkers and bosses will remember how you took the bad news and will remember your strength in dealing with it.

2. *Show an Attitude of Gratitude*
   This is a tough one, but it needs to be done to ensure a solid reputation with your coworkers, HR representative, and bosses. Make sure you show your appreciation for having had the opportunity to work for these people. Let your coworkers know you enjoyed working with them and appreciated what they may have done for you. And let your boss know you learned valuable lessons from them, and try to be empathetic for what he and the company may be going through. If you have any unfinished projects, bring your team up to speed on what needs to be done to carry out the necessary steps. Stomping out the door and yelling "You can figure it all out!" won't serve you well down the road. Handle the situation with grace and your attitude and consideration during a tough time will be well remembered.

3. *Don't Have a Major Pity Party*
   The first thing people usually say when something like this happens is, "Why me?" Don't start comparing yourself to others in the department who were not let go. Don't walk out the door with a sour expression or make a condescending remark to a person in the department who was not given a pink slip. Fear is your biggest enemy right now, but you must try to calm the enemy down. It doesn't matter why someone was spared who you feel wasn't as good a worker as you. What matters is your next move toward a better place in your life. Many people of high position have been fired and gone on to bigger and better

things. In a few months, you might look back at this and say, "Thank you!"

4. *Maintain Good Relationships with Former Coworkers*
Your best leads usually come from people who know you and know how you work. Also, as big as the industry is, it's actually quite small. Your next boss might be playing golf with your old boss one day and bring your name up. It's to your advantage to keep in touch with people who may be able to help you in your job search. Also, company reps might attend association conferences or conventions in the industry and hear about a lead they could pass on to you. Having a former colleague or boss speak positively about you and how you handled yourself on termination day might be the tie breaker between you and another candidate in a competitive market. Companies look at everything under a microscope these days. Make sure when they look at you, they see class, professionalism, and good grooming Those are qualities that the best companies look for in addition to skills and education. Make sure your professional character is flawless and highly regarded.

5. *Make Job Searching Your New Full-Time Job*
You must consider this process a full-time job and have a strategy and plan. Reach out to coworkers and recruiters who specialize in your industry, and make sure your LinkedIn profile is updated and impressive. Also, make sure any other social media you work with, including Facebook and Twitter, have only the most professional posts and pictures. Your image now must be only the most professional it can possibly be. People have lost job offers because of a questionable post on Facebook. Don't take the chance that such a thing might happen to you. It has been said that activity generates activity. You need to spend most of the day talking to people on the phone, researching on the computer, and attending networking functions in your area. The more you do, the better your chances of getting interviews and offers. And make sure your resume is as professional as

possible. Many large corporations are using digital methods to screen resumes, so you must have language that will get their attention. Misspelled words and bad grammar can be a kiss of death in this process. If you need to spend money with a professional resume service, don't hesitate. It will be well worth the investment.

6. *Tighten Your Belt*

   If you were lucky enough to get a severance package, it will eventually run out. If not, then you have to tug on that belt fast. Look at your lifestyle and see what you can live without. Maybe not going out to eat with friends isn't the end of the world. In many cases, friends might be out of work as well, and a good meatloaf or potluck dinner can bring more people together and assure a continued connection. Support is always a good thing at times like this. A big fat steak dinner at a fancy steakhouse with a double dollop of sour cream on your baked potato twice a week isn't great for your waistline, anyway. Maybe the situation will force you to get into better shape and have a more positive self-image. A positive self-image is always a positive on an interview. If you feel good about yourself, the prospective employer can feel it. And studies have shown that self-assured people tend to make better employees.

7. *Welcome Change*

   It could be that the situation is a real blessing in disguise. Often, we don't do any real soul-searching until we are forced to. We don't grow when we are complacent; we stagnate. Sometimes a job change is just the recipe for a rebirth. Put your arms around this new challenge and embrace it. You might look back in years to come and be glad it happened. Look at the rules of nature. In winter, the plants are dormant and not blossoming fruit. Without rain, those plants can't grow and bear new fruit in the spring.

My hope is that those of you who are reading this have not been laid off or fired. But if this has happened or should happen to you, or if you know of someone going through this, remember the many successful entrepreneurs who have failed over and over again and come out stronger and better as human beings. Your attitude will determine your altitude. Make sure yours is one that will soar higher than you could ever imagine. And look at this as your opportunity to become the best you can be. In his book on creating success, Napoleon Hill (2012) states that "every adversity brings with it the seed of an equivalent advantage," and that "every failure brings with it the seed of an equivalent success." Let that be your new mantra.

As an executive recruiter with thirty years of experience, I have survived five separate economic downturns in Houston. Although the current downturn is somewhat unique and may last far longer than its predecessors, you *can* survive if you cultivate the correct mindset. Those who survive will emerge from this situation stronger, wiser, and with a renewed sense of self and purpose. So don't look upon your past failures, particularly those that might have occurred because of a market downturn, as final judgments. Instead, look for ways to succeed despite the current situation.

There are thousands of factors that have created this perfect storm of a spiraling job market. But eventually the waves will calm, the tides will recede, and the industries we work in will right themselves again. What matters most is this: Who will *you* be when the change comes? How can you *use* this time to reevaluate and recalibrate your professional skills, passions, and commitments? The steps of The Faremouth Method help you *act* when the world around you is simply *reacting*. So roll up your sleeves and get busy. If you are determined to survive this storm and emerge stronger and smarter, then you will have to take the lead.

Step Back or Step Up?

We all, at some point in our lives, will have a setback. I had one recently when I found out a good friend of over fifteen years died of pancreatic cancer. She was a gifted and talented woman who put her dreams into motion. Barbara was a well-known hairdresser who owned many beauty shops and wanted to expand her business to make and develop hair products. She worked with a chemist and put out a popular brand of hair products and then wrote a book about how her trade allowed her to help others improve their self-image and self-esteem. Her life was cut short at fifty-three years of age, but even so, I applaud her for stepping back, evaluating where she wanted to go, taking a major risk, and fulfilling her dreams.

When we experience any type of death, whether it be an actual death, the death of a career, job loss, or the ending of a relationship, we can look at it as a major setback, or perhaps as taking a step back, to look at ourselves and determine what comes next. Sometimes a setback is just the thump on the head we need to regroup, revamp our goals, and move forward when we've been stalled for a long time. I must admit that most of my day, after hearing about her death, was filled with sadness and grief over losing a friend. But this death also made me step back and take a good hard look at some important areas of my own life.

When you experience a setback in your own life, give yourself some time to grieve, but also use the time to step back and honestly review what comes next. It may be an opportunity to look deep inside yourself and align yourself with a new passion, goal, or way of life that will allow you to grow and develop. It's all in how you look at things. A step back might allow you to step forward into a whole new way of life.

It All Starts with Self-Love

So often, we look outside ourselves for fulfillment. I've heard people say, "If only I found the right person to share my life with, I would be happy." But would you really? If you don't know and love yourself first, some other person or event in your life won't make it happen. And for some more than others, this process could take years or even a lifetime to accomplish. Some people go to their grave without self-love. And self-love is not something that just happens, either. Sometimes, accomplishments or lots of failures can help us get closer to unlocking the inner door that allows us look deep within ourselves to find self-love.

As an employment counselor, my job is to assess people and assist them in finding careers that will utilize their strengths and abilities. Time and again, I've looked at the high achievers in life and realized that those who accomplish great things in life can do so because they love themselves. These are the trailblazers. I read something on Facebook from an old friend once that set me on this bandwagon. It said something about how you can be a good person and people will still criticize you. I was compelled to write a comment to this person: "Who cares? If you know who and what you are, it shouldn't matter what someone else thinks." It spoke volumes to me that this person was looking for validation outside of himself. He was giving his power away. And many people do it. But I suppose the real question is, how does a person begin to love himself? What is the formula for self-love?

I'm not sure I know the perfect answer to this question. However, Tess Marshall (2011) reflects on this idea in her *Tiny Buddha* article "21 Tips to Release Self-Neglect and Love Yourself in Action." "The most important decision of your life, the one that will affect every other decision you make, is the commitment to love and accept yourself. It directly affects the quality of your relationships, your work, your free time, your faith, and your future." She lists twenty-one steps to help you "discover your worth and enfold yourself in affection and appreciation." The following five relate most easily to loving yourself on your journey to finding a new job:

1. *Begin your day with love (not technology).*
   Before rising for the day, take time to remember that you are worthy of the world and what you strive for. Instead of picking up your phone to check your text messages, simply lie in bed and breathe. Set your intentions for the day and program your mind to be grateful and positive.

2. *Take time to meditate and journal daily.*
   Think about what you want the day to look like and write down your goals. Spend five minutes before getting out of bed in

meditation. Starting the day focused on inner reflection rather than outer reflection can help us remain true to ourselves in the face of negative outward stimuli.

3. *Expand your interests.*
   Look for new things to try and continue learning. Make a commitment to investigate available classes or groups you might be interested in joining. These could expand your knowledge base and make you a more well-rounded individual.

4. *Own your potential.*
   The opportunities available to you are limitless. Applaud yourself for the great excel spreadsheet you put out at the last minute or the important deadline you were able to meet because of your experience level. Giving yourself a pat on the back every once in a while can boost your confidence and allow you to really love who you are.

5. *Live in appreciation.*
   Have an attitude of gratitude. Acknowledge and cherish that which makes you talented, beautiful, and brilliant. Focus on what you have rather than what you lack. Whatever we focus on expands. So why not make your focus one that is more positive so you can bring more positive vibrations into your life?

For some people, lots of trial and error might be necessary to find out who they are and what gives them joy. And as we grow up, our needs and desires do change. I suppose the courage to fail must be mentioned here. If you decided on a job that doesn't turn out to be your dream job, it's okay. You will still learn valuable lessons from the experience and perhaps get closer to finding out who you are and what is important to you. What is the old saying: "nothing ventured, nothing gained"? Maybe having the courage to do it anyway, even if you are not 100 percent certain it's the perfect position for you, is what is necessary. Self-love is a process. Get out there, and give it your best shot. If it doesn't work out, realize that you have grown from the experience, and it will probably put you in touch with who you really are and allow you to learn about your strengths and abilities. Loving yourself is critical to putting you on the right path. Stay positive, and do not let life's ups and downs tear you apart. Love yourself every single day, no matter what. That's the key to finding true success in any area of your life.

CHAPTER 6

FOR THE EMPLOYER

Is Your Company Feeling the Talent Drought?

The talent drought you are probably feeling as an employer is serious. And it's only going to get worse. As an executive recruiter for many years, I feel your pain. Every day, I get calls from employers complaining that they can't find qualified people to fill their open jobs. And analysts predict that, by the year 2020, we will have a global problem. Large economies, including Russia, Canada, South Korea, and China, will have more people at retirement age than are entering the workforce.

According to an article recently published in the Harvard Business Review, there are three factors contributing to this problem: globalization, demographics, and, most importantly, the leadership pipeline (Fernández-Aráoz 2014). The leadership pipeline is an area I have taken great interest in, and I have found that such a challenge is widespread throughout many industries. Many companies and businesses simply don't have a strong enough leadership pipeline; they don't have a surplus of potential, talented leaders with a long-term investment in the longevity and health of the company. It's a global problem. And the only way to solve it is to make more-intelligent, durable hires, matching the right people with the right positions at the right time. The Faremouth Method can work in any industry and for a wide variety of positions currently available to be filled.

Five Steps of The Faremouth Method
Steps for the Employer

To determine the type of person who will fit your company best, you must first understand your company culture and how different types of people would fit within it. Experience and intelligence are no longer the only, or even the most important, credentials to secure in a candidate. Instead, emotional intelligence paired with a passion for the job tends to be a better predictor for a right fit and long-term employment.

According to the World Economic Forum's 2016 Future of Jobs Report, emotional intelligence will be one of the top ten job skills in 2020 (Leopold, Ratcheva, and Zahidi 2016). In a 2011 CareerBuilder Survey of more than 2,600 hiring managers and HR professionals, 71 percent stated they valued emotional intelligence in an employee over IQ; 75 percent would promote a worker with high emotional intelligence over others; and 59 percent claimed they would pass up a candidate with a high IQ but low emotional intelligence (CareerBuilder 2011). Here are seven of the top reasons why candidates with high emotional intelligence are so valuable:

1. They cope better with pressure.

2. They are good at teamwork.

3. They tend to be good listeners.

4. They are open to feedback.

5. They are empathetic.

6. They make good role models.

7. They think decisions through before making them.

Step 1. Do a Self-Inventory

We are in changing times—times that force us to use different methods to solve our hiring problems. There is a real shortage of experienced talent available to hiring managers. And alternative methods of hiring must be implemented. How can we reduce the odds of making a bad hire when the candidates we are interviewing don't have the exact skill set we need for the jobs we are trying to fill?

The answer to this important question begins with having a clear understanding of what the job entails and clarifying expectations before the candidate is hired. If the interviewer clearly understands the mechanics of the job, then an accomplished high achiever can often transfer previous success to the task at hand. What are your company's core values? What is your mission? Your best bet is to seek both conventional and unconventional candidates who align with that mission.

It's in asking the right questions and observing previously demonstrated achievements that you reduce the risk of making a bad hire.

Step 2. Ask Better Questions

A company can begin to ask better questions by conducting a job-history review to look for the Accomplishment/Achievement Patterns I wrote about in chapter four.

You can also gather important information by asking nontraditional interview questions. In other words, ask the candidates questions they may not have prepared answers for (for example, *can you tell me about a difficult situation you may have had with a supervisor and how you handled it?*) (Murphy 2011). Maybe the candidate's answers will demonstrate a problem-solving attitude: "My boss was focused on in-person contacts, while I was more into contact management systems. We met in the middle. I tried to understand where he was coming from, and as a result, we were able to use his long-tenured client relationships with the technological innovations I suggested to operate more efficiently and tap into client referrals." Or perhaps the candidate will provide a more revealing answer: "My boss was living in the caveman ages. He didn't do anything modern and up-to-date, and it was frustrating to work with him. I ended up going to a competitor, because his old-fashioned ways of doing business made me crazy." Such an answer demonstrates a prospective employee who is all about themselves and perhaps not willing to see both sides of a situation. They might be a difficult employee to manage, especially if your staff is more on the senior-tenured employee end as opposed to technology-based millennials. Look for the *problem-solver* message in response to such a question. On the other hand, a red flag would be a candidate playing the blame game—when all you hear in response to such a question is bashing of another person or that it was always someone else's problem.

Step 3. Step Out of Your Comfort Zone

As employers, we must be willing, in this new market, to take calculated risks. If you have always hired a degreed person with two years of inside sales experience in your industry, you might consider hiring a person who is non-degreed or degreed in a totally unrelated area with experience in a related field who has demonstrated success. I had a candidate who had success written all over him, but his degree was in health sciences and he had worked at a sporting-goods store. I knew he had a burning desire to get into the oil and gas business, but his experience was in a far-removed field. His degree, however, had a science base to it, and his track record of success and stability told me this young man was worth taking a chance on. All his friends were in the oil and gas business in companies that could perhaps help him down the road in the oil and gas arena. And without exact experience, he wasn't able to command the high dollars that experienced candidates could. The president of the company was a person who knew and respected me and trusted my opinion. He knew that in a time of slower business, he could take the time to train the candidate, benefit from the lower salary, and hopefully reap the benefits of a good hire. He ended up hiring my candidate, who has turned out to be a great employee. He has been promoted from inside to outside sales and has even been able to do deals with some of his friends in other related industries. It was a win-win for all parties. It was a risk, but again, it was a calculated risk that seemed to be worth it. Had the president not been willing to step out of his comfort zone and hire in an alternative way, this success story could never have been realized.

Step 4. Take Your Time and Do It Right

There is no magic timeframe for taking the time to do it right when it comes to a company hiring an employee. Many factors need to be considered when going through this process. If you are working with a skilled recruiter, they will often perform the necessary reference and background checks, which can save the in-house corporate recruiter time. But to make a solid placement, the company needs to make sure many things are in alignment. Does the applicant to be hired fit in with the team? If they are a millennial and the others in the departments are baby boomers, can they work well together and perhaps blend the skills of both groups to ensure a positive outcome? Is the person's tenure solid, and if not, are their reasons for leaving previous jobs good ones? What are the goals of both parties? If the applicant to be hired wants to be in a management role in two years, is that a real potentiality? Rushing the process because the person looks good on paper, has been highly recommended by a client, or conducts a dynamite first interview is taking a big risk in today's market.

I once had a client take an applicant to lunch. Ahead of time, he planned for the waiter to mess up the applicant's order; he felt he would be able to see how the applicant handled a challenge when things went wrong. Up until that point, the applicant had passed through the interviews with flying colors. But when his order came out all wrong, the applicant got very upset with the waiter. He acted rudely, told the waiter he wasn't too smart, and got really ugly in front of his potential boss. After the lunch experience, my client decided not to hire the candidate. He called me and told me that if the applicant acted this way with a waiter, he would probably do the same with a customer, and my client could not take the chance of losing a customer in this tight market because of poor customer service. The client took the time to do it right and went the extra mile with the lunch meeting. It gave him valuable information that may have saved him from making a very bad hiring decision.

Step 5. Be a Hunter

As employers in this new market situation, you need to be more aggressive in your efforts to hire the right candidates. You must hunt for experienced talent. Be more proactive than you've been in the past, consider different methods, and make sure your hunt for the right talent is utilizing the right steps. You can't just put an ad on a job board and expect all the applicants to meet your current needs. You have to go after talent in a way that you may never have before. Seek out talent on your own through your own job postings, or hunt for the best professional recruiter, whether in-house or third party, to assist you in your search. If you want a trophy candidate, you cannot keep hunting where you will only find mediocre candidates. They are out there, and with the right tools and strategies, you will ensure that you are making the absolute best hire for your company.

Five Tips for Keeping the Best

With the current talent shortage, employers must be more aware of practices to implement to retain good employees. It is important, now more than ever, to boost employee satisfaction and productivity, and to make sure your organization is doing the right things to not lose your high achievers and keep them motivated to succeed. Just giving them big raises and bonuses isn't enough. As employers, we need to be proactive in our efforts to understand the needs of our employees and keep them with our company. With all the jobs available in our marketplace, it's crucial to our organizational success to take steps to ensure long-term retention.

Stellar employees are not simply motivated by money. Yes, promotions and pay raises do provide a sense of success and status. But the employees of today's workforce crave a deeper meaning at work beyond their paycheck.

We all need to feel appreciated, important, and that our contributions matter. By utilizing the following five strategies, you can provide your team members with the motivation and support they need to continue to be excited about their job and enable them to provide outstanding results.

1. Listen to Your Employees

Active listening is important. Everyone needs to feel they are appreciated for their ideas. We as human beings need to feel we matter and that our contributions are important. At a recent seminar I attended, Oprah stressed how we all have the same basic needs. She discussed how, in all her years of interviewing different types of people, including national presidents, the first thing they asked her once the interview was over was "Did I do okay?" We all need validation. Let your staff speak out about their experiences working for your company and encourage them to freely present insights, suggestions, and new methods of doing business. Be mindful that the environment in which this is conducted is safe and that appropriate steps will be considered to improve conditions in the work environment. The key here is to make sure your team members feel their ideas are heard and valued. Making employees feel their ideas matter are important ingredients to building a productive team. Also, passionate workers stay with the company longer, produce better quality work, and inspire other workers in the organization.

2. Celebrate Your Employees' Accomplishments

Setting clear common goals for teams to work toward is crucial to encouraging your employees to stay focused and perform well. Providing tangible rewards for goal achievement is an effective tool to ensure high productivity. A well-known chain of hair salons I have visited for over twenty years has amazing retention rates. One of the stylists has been with the salon for over thirty years and other stylists have long tenure as well. The salon provides their high achievers with two luxury trips a year. They also reward their high achievers with expensive gifts for their contribution to the salon and high productivity. They have frequent employee staff celebrations on birthdays, holidays, and special personal events. This builds a sense of community among the employees and makes coming to work fun. And you can feel the positive energy when you enter the salon. It makes for a positive experience for the customers when they enter such an upbeat environment.

3. Allow Employees to Choose Their Work

A project we find interesting challenges our psyche. Take the time to speak with your employees and determine what encourages them to work hard. By allowing your employees to choose, you are not only allowing them to focus on their passions but also showing them your investment in their success and happiness with the company. Making your employees feel supported and valued is key to keeping productivity high. Make time to sit down with your employees and understand what they want to do as employees of your company. This also gives them incentive to progress and make valuable contributions to your company's growth.

4. Recognize Individuals Publicly

Implementing recognition strategies to acknowledge individuals who deserve extra praise for hard work and company contributions is crucial to keeping up morale. Having a Most Valuable Player award or awarding a hundred-dollar gift card can go a long way in employee satisfaction in the workplace. It also gives others on the team motivation to achieve goals and work hard for similar recognition. Friendly competition is a good thing. A verbal pat on the back is an effective tool to encourage people to achieve and grow.

5. Create a Positive Work Environment

A positive attitude is imperative in the work day. Creating positive energy in the work environment by celebrating professional and personal milestones goes a long way to making people want to come to work. And we all need to feel we are special and cared about. A few years ago, a young man I placed had a very difficult situation; his two-year-old son had been diagnosed with leukemia. The executives of the company ran a fundraiser with various activities to help the young man pay for his huge medical expenses. Not only did this make the employee feel supported and cared about, it also built a sense of community among the employees. The child went into remission, but the young man was so grateful for the company's efforts to assist him with his challenge that he became fully invested with the company and became a top performer.

Money isn't enough to ensure retention among your staff. Having the personal element in the workplace is often worth more than a big raise in the paycheck. In understanding our employees' passions and human needs, and appreciating people for their own uniqueness, we can motivate our employees to become top performers. Happy workers are productive workers. Productive workers make the company money, and if they are happy and working hard, the monetary rewards usually follow.

The Top Five Mistakes Employers Make

Each business, company, employer, and business culture is unique, but there are a few things employers do regularly that keep them from achieving their hiring and retention goals:

1. *They hire for an old job or one that is not current with market conditions.*
   As an employer, you need to be cognizant of updated technology, such as contact management systems, that would allow you to streamline your processes. You can't expect a millennial employee to make fifty cold calls in the same way baby boomer employees once did. In addition, if your particular industry is in a downturn, you might need to consider hiring one candidate with a multifaceted skill set that can handle a variety of duties, while in the past you might have had two people doing the same job.

2. *They low-ball offers and have heavy turnover or lose good candidates to the competition.*
   Employers need to seriously consider the big picture. To lose a candidate that could have greatly affected the bottom line is

a bigger loss to the company than a salary range that may be 10–20% more than what they originally wanted to pay. In fact, I see situations all the time where a $10K hike in salary could have brought the company $10 million in new sales because of the relationships and book of business the candidate could have brought in the door.

3. *The client waits too long to make an offer and loses the candidate.*
    Sometimes employers are afraid to pull the trigger and hire a candidate. And often the candidate finds another opportunity elsewhere, leaving both sides with a bad taste in their mouths. These such companies may need to streamline their interviewing processes to better compile all the information they need to make a good decision. New techniques, such as asking for references or utilizing behavioral questions during interviews, may be necessary to expedite the process of making an offer.

4. *The company doesn't examine the real reason for heavy turnover.*
    Heavy turnover can be caused by many things, but sometimes employers play the blame game—blaming an HR rep, the recruiting company, the market—instead of taking ownership of the problem, solving it, and moving on. Such companies might consider passing out confidential employee evaluation forms at the time of performance reviews to get employee input about internal processes that could be improved. This could bring to light internal situations that management may not be aware of. Using such knowledge to improve the situation could help make the company a better place to work.

5. *They don't take the time or invest the money to make a good hire in the beginning.*
    The company decides to hire in the old way and only looks at paper—matching resume to job description. They don't get under the hood of the resume to determine if the candidate is a good match for the company culture, has the right work ethic, and has skills that can either be expanded or immediately

utilized. Also, they may only use technology—such as word searches—to make a hire and not consider the human element.

Hiring Millennials vs. Baby Boomers

The way we hire has to change. Or perhaps it's our mindset about hiring that must change. We now have essentially two different groups of employees seeking employment, and the way they look at the world and approach work is significantly different. If employers are not willing to take a hard look at the differences between these groups—the millennials and the baby boomers—they will make costly hiring mistakes and have enormous turnover.

Angela Duckworth, in her fascinating book *Grit*, writes that:

> research shows that people are enormously more satisfied with their jobs when they do something that fits their personal interests. This is the conclusion of a meta-analysis that aggregated data from almost a hundred different studies that collectively included working adults in just about every conceivable profession. For instance, people who enjoy thinking about abstract ideas are *not* happy managing the minutiae of logistically complicated projects; they'd rather be solving math problems. And people who really enjoy interacting with people are *not* happy when their job is to work alone at a computer all day; they're much better off in jobs like sales or teaching. What's more, people whose jobs match their personal interests are, in general, happier with their lives as a whole.

> Second, people *perform* better at work when what they do interests them. This is the conclusion of another meta-analysis of sixty studies conducted over the past sixty years. Employees whose intrinsic personal interests fit with their occupations do their jobs better, are more helpful to their coworkers, and stay at their jobs longer. (2016, 97)

It's certainly true that you can't get a job just doing *anything* you enjoy. It's tough to make a living playing Frisbee, no matter how good you get at it. And there are a lot of people in the world whose circumstances preclude the luxury of choosing among a broad array of occupational options. Like it or not, there are real constraints in the choices we can make about how we earn a living. If Tom has an elderly father who is in assisted living and he is the only child, he can't take a sales job that has him traveling 60 percent of the time. Of course, employers can't ask these personal questions, but if he's a baby boomer, this scenario could quite possibly be the case.

As an employer, you have probably seen the evidence that people make better employees if their jobs are aligned with their interests and passions. But how can you make the best hiring decision, let's say, if your millennial supervisor of sales of a newly merged company inherits a seasoned baby boomer employee who has been with the company for fifteen years. They both have personal interests and strong needs in a job, but the ways they go about actualizing those work needs are different.

I once had a situation brought to my attention concerning this very scenario. The ending of the story did not turn out well at all. Perhaps if both parties had understood the differences of these two groups, and the VP of the company had read this book *before* the merger took place, this story could have had a different ending.

Aggravated Anthony was referred to me by a long-standing client of mine. Aggravated Anthony had just quit his job of fifteen years because his company had recently merged with a larger conglomerate and brought in all new management. Aggravated Anthony happened to be a baby boomer and had been successful in his sales career handling his job with a baby boomer work ethic. His new boss, Tony the Tiger Millennial, had Ivy League credentials and had been recruited off campus three years before to become the manager of this large conglomerate as part of the "change management" practices to bring the company up-to-speed with technology and recent market conditions. Aggravated Anthony and Tony the Tiger were like oil and water working together. They just didn't mix, and they did not communicate well. The VP, who had been with the newly purchased division for his entire career, didn't see the writing on the wall concerning this disaster waiting to happen. Had he understood the differences in mindset and work styles of these two different groups, he might not have lost a valuable employee in Aggravated Anthony.

When Anthony came to me, making a salary of over $150K, and told me he quit his job because he didn't get along with his new millennial boss, I almost fell off my chair. The market he was coming into in his industry was not doing well. Layoffs were continuing to happen and because of the surplus of applicants, salaries in the industry were at an all-time low.

If you are an employer reading this chapter, then keep in mind the following three factors that might have led to the breakdown in this case. If handled differently, they might have led to a more positive outcome:

Three Factors that Cause a Breakdown between Millennials and Baby Boomers

1. Millennials are, in most cases, more about technology, while baby boomers are more about communication. If the management of this team had recognized these differences and discussed how each is necessary to the whole of the team, a compromise could have been worked out. If Aggravated Anthony could have taken his book of business and relationships to his new boss and shared his style of maintaining trust and building relationships with his customers, and Tony the Tiger could have instructed him how to put them all into his contact management list, they both could have benefited from the exchange of information.

2. Millennials are more about work/life balance, while baby boomers are all about long hours and getting the job done. Anthony had been with the company for fifteen years and reported to work at 7:00 every morning, while his new boss, Tony, came in at 8:05 after working out at the gym in his spinning class. Anthony became resentful that he was now supervised by someone who didn't have the same work ethic he did. If the VP had had an informal meeting

or dinner bringing these two together and discussing their work ethic differences, there might have been less resentment and more understanding on Anthony's end.

3. Millennials are more about social media, technology, instant gratification, connection, communication, and team approach, while in most cases, baby boomers like to handle the "whole enchilada" and see a project from inception to completion and get credit for a job well done. Baby boomers may also at times be afraid of being put out to pasture and be more reluctant to let go of the reins of projects. Anthony was concerned about not being seen as the "main gun" anymore, but after resigning, he became the "Lone Ranger," trying to find a job in a tough market, with no money coming in. When a job offer was made, he would probably be forced to take a huge pay cut. If he had tried to learn how to relate to his current boss, he might have stay employed and not had the increased stress of trying to find a job in a challenging market.

Having a clear understanding of the differences in mindsets and work ethics of both these groups gives employers enormous power and the ability to do preventative maintenance to avoid losing valuable employees. Neither of these groups is entirely wrong or right. There is simply a significant difference in generational mindsets that we all need to be aware of when we hire. Also, we need to consider a blending of these two groups in our organizations. Who knows, perhaps hiring a baby boomer candidate with experience and relationships to work with the tech-savvy millennial is an option your organization should consider. Generational differences can be a huge opportunity for your company, and technology is here to stay. If we aren't set up to embrace these challenges, we put ourselves into a dangerous situation for the future.

Now is the time to build up and not break down. By working together and sharing what we know with clarity, humor, and purpose, we can solve our hiring needs and emerge stronger than we were before.

Employer Assessment Tests

Many of the tests client companies use for assessment are specific to their company culture as well as the type of position for which they are screening. For example, a different test is utilized to fill a sales position than is used to fill an engineering or technical role. The tests measure a variety of skills, and the clients need to determine which test is best available to give them the information they need for their company culture and position.

1. *The Brooks Group (www.brooksgroup.com)*
   This test is helpful, as it points to both the training and the coaching an individual might need based on their results. It combines three assessments into one application. They measure values, behavior, and attitudes. The tools that help you select a person will also help manage them and train them based on their individual needs.

2. *Smart Work Assessments (www.smartworkassessments.com)*
   Smart Work Assessments provides several assessment categories, depending on the career, to help you make the best hire. They provide recommendations on mentors and provide simple interview questions to help you better understand the applicant.

3. *The Myers-Briggs (www.myersbriggs.org)*
   The MBTI is a psychometric questionnaire designed to measure psychological preferences of how people view the world and make decisions. It shows that behavior is quite orderly and consistent, due to the basic differences in the way an individual prefers to use their perceptions and judgment. Perception is becoming aware of things, people, happenings, or ideas. Judgment is making a conclusion about what has been perceived.

4. *Berke (www.berkeassessment.com)*
   This is a five-step test that helps you know if a candidate is right for your company. (1) You begin by describing the job, such as

what it involves, the key tasks, and the more challenging activities. (2) You then set the job target to identify the core behaviors and talents you will need to secure the right candidate. This will help the assessment understand where you can compromise. (3) The assessment then measures the personality traits, natural talents, and intelligence of the candidate taking it. (4) The assessment gives you a report that helps you discern whether the candidate is a match for the position. (5) The final step brings up challenges and discusses strategies for handling them.

5. *Birkman (www.birkman.com)*
    This test helps determine the candidate's strengths, expectations, stress behaviors, and motivations, which can lead to choosing the best candidate for your role. It also helps you understand people's skills and puts together roles and relationships for higher productivity and success.

As you may have noticed, some of these tests are available to both applicants and employers. I have only mentioned two in this chapter, those being the Myers-Briggs and the Birkman assessments. Again, there are many other assessments available both to candidates and employers. Throughout my career as a recruiting specialist, I have even known companies who have had customized tests developed specifically for them. I have also had clients who used a trained psychologist to interpret results with both applicants and employers. No matter what though, remember that people are a variable product. Situations, such as traumatic experiences, deaths in the family, emotional challenges, etc., can influence assessment responses, so tread carefully when interpreting their results.

There are pros and cons to every practice, and assessment tests are no different. Some pros are that the results are quantifiable and the assessments are timely and cost-effective. Some cons are that the scores might be influenced by external factors, such as fatigue, and the questions are often general in nature.

Finding the Right Recruiter to Meet Your Needs

The onset of the technology age has been of real value to this group of professionals for the last thirty years. Since the 1990s, we have been gifted with the internet and many available resources. With the new, younger generation of the workforce, this tool is ingrained in their way of communicating. This sector of the market is a captive audience for technology, and statistics have demonstrated that a large part of their day is spent on one or more of these devices. Job boards are everywhere, and most people looking for a job are checking these areas all the time. Job boards, LinkedIn, and postings on professional association boards are all tools utilized by recruiters every day. But do these resources tell you all you need to know to make a hire that will align with your corporate culture and allow you to make the best match? When a client company interviews a prospective recruiter, they should ask them how they find their candidates. Do they take the time to conduct their job in a creative way? Do they do actual recruiting to secure good people? If you ask them "How do you find the good candidates?" and their response is "I post ads on job boards," does that assure you that you are on the right path?

A recruiter must engage in different methods these days to secure a candidate who will be a good match for your needs. They must think outside the box in this challenging market to tap into resources that might be foreign to traditional hiring methods. They must demonstrate to you that they "walk the walk," and you should conduct checks on your end to see if they are in fact working in your best interest. These suggestions are critical to securing a recruiting consultant who will find you a long-term candidate and make you proud to have secured their services.

Also, ask about their tenure in the profession and whether they are members of professional recruiting associations. Belonging to an organization with a code of ethics and outlined principles of professionalism goes a long way. Do they have any certifications, degrees, or published articles? Do they attend continuing education programs to keep them up-to-date with professional practices in their field? Paying a sizable fee, only to realize in six months that the person you hired has gone on to bigger and better things, is a wasted investment of time and money.

And continue to dig deeper. Ask them for five or more references of notable companies who have used their services. If they can't give you at least five references, you might not be dealing with the most seasoned of recruiters.

Also, find out what they most enjoy doing on their days off and what hobbies they have? If they tell you they enjoy spending time with family and are involved with community service-oriented activities, it could give you an insight into their integral fiber and makeup. Integrity is multidimensional. It's blended into many areas of a human being's life. Your time and money is not something you take lightly. Take the time to make sure you are working with a person who will give you value for your investment.

Trust and consideration are also important traits to evaluate. If they seem to skim over things and not give you sound, reasonable answers to your questions, keep asking more questions. A fast, smooth-talking recruiter is often a dangerous one. I once had a recruiter tell me for fifteen minutes all the important people they knew. They made sure I was aware of their prestigious contacts, which brought up a huge red flag for me. I didn't care who they knew; I wanted to know what they knew and who they were. This recruiter ended up giving me a falsified reference. I happened to know the person they got the reference from, and that person had never even talked to them.

As I have said in previous chapters, make sure you ask the right questions to ensure you will be delivered an honest, sincere, and genuine service. You deserve that. And you will be happy you took the time on the front-end to learn the important information that can make your hiring experience a good one.

Ten Steps to Keep Employees Motivated
during Tough Times

When times are tough, everyone in the company is nervous. Good managers must strive to help employees stay focused, engaged, and motivated. An email saying "Stay upbeat; we've been through five of these downturns and we are still in business" is not enough. No pat on the back or simple team-building exercise completely uplifts workplace confidence. During the writing of this chapter, I am experiencing employees panicking in a slumping economic climate and picking up the phone to call my agency to see what stable opportunities might be available. Here are ten steps that might benefit employers and discourage their employees from making those calls:

1. *Don't Let Stress Turn You into a Drill Sergeant*
    Employees can feel the stress of their supervisor, and it trickles down, even to the mail clerk. Make sure you are taking adequate measures to blow off steam and stress in productive ways, and try not to bring it into the office. If you need to go longer on the treadmill early in the morning, do it. If it means you read uplifting reports rather than focus on all the doom and gloom, then make it happen. Whatever you do or don't do, make sure your interaction with your employees is positive, upbeat, and determined.

2. *Keep Your Door Open*
    Many employees have reported to me that they were getting nervous because more and more closed-door meetings were taking place. They were concerned that their superiors were planning another layoff or something similar. If you must have a roundtable with your managers, consider going out of the office to do it. Keep your door open as much as possible, and make your employees feel like their input and concern about the challenging market is your concern as well. Let them feel they can come into your office to discuss the business climate. Make them feel welcome, valued, and supported.

3. *Recognize and Praise Hard Work*

When business is down or slow, it's even more important to focus on praising your employees. When employees understand that their efforts are noticed during tough times, they will usually continue to put forth the effort. Even if they make twenty-five cold calls and get twenty-five "Nos," supporting their efforts and encouraging them to continue to reach out to customers, even if they don't land a sale right away, encourages them to not lose faith or get discouraged.

4. *Assist Employees in Fulfilling Career Goals*

In down cycles, it's even more important to sit down with employees to understand their long-term goals. Talk with them about perhaps rotating into other departments to broaden their experience, give them new projects with more responsibility, encourage them to take on research projects to find what other markets may need products, etc. If their long-term goals require additional education or advanced degrees, visit with them about tuition reimbursement options or online programs that may be available. If there are grant or scholarship options available, assist them in planning and researching what programs may be available for them. The support and consideration you show them, especially in tough times, goes a long way.

5. *Break Up the Negative Huddle*

If you notice you have two disgruntled employees feeding each other and poisoning their work environment, try to break them apart and move them away from each other. Negativity breeds more negativity.

6. *Stop the Bleeding*

Try to interrupt rumors and explain to the employees where the future is headed, if possible. When employees are bombarded by media, TV, and negativity in the workplace, try to stop it before it gets out of hand.

7. *Plan Ahead*
   Set longer-term goals for all employees. Down cycles eventually come to an end. Talk about ideas for expanding growth when the market does turn around.

8. *Sponsor Events Outside of the Office*
   Get out of the office and sponsor events that encourage team building. When employees feel that management is investing in them to have a positive, uplifting experience, it can go a long way in the morale department. As Robert Safian (2017) points out, "nothing builds bonds like looking someone in the eye, laughing together or crying together, or just plain talking through ideas together."

9. *Keep Your Major Concerns about the Market to Yourself*
   The worst thing you can do is share concerns about the business climate with employees. It can set the tone for panic and push them to seek more secure ground. Not that you should become Bozo the Clown and act like all is wonderful and great in the marketplace. But watch your words and what you say to employees during tough times.

10. *List the Positive Outcomes of Other Down Cycles You've Been Through*
    Focus on finding the light in the darkness. If you've been through other downturns, demonstrate how lessons learned and customer bonding during slow times ended up being a positive move to beat the competition when the market finally turned around.

Make your employees feel supported during these tough times. Showing your support and gratitude, and encouraging them to grow and expand, goes a long way toward retaining good folks and building a work environment that will attract other excellent employees. Retaining good employees through tough times is as important, if not more so, than attracting new people to your company. Your current employees are your greatest assets. Make sure you are not encouraging them to expand without you!

Seven Rules for Creating a Work Culture
of Passionate Employees

Business is all about cycles. In any industry, we have our up cycles and our down ones. When we are in the midst of a down cycle, it's even more critical to have "A" players, cut the fat, and evaluate our corporate culture. For the long-term viability of any enterprise, you need a viable corporate culture. A corporate culture that reflects your company's true values is of paramount importance for long-term success. Surrounding yourself with good people and being able to retain them is a company goal. Keep in mind these seven rules for creating the right conditions to reflect your company's creed:

1. *The Right People Need to Be Hired*
    Hire for passion and commitment first, experience second, and credentials third. Impressive resumes are plentiful, but you should try to find people who are interested in the same things you are. Being merely a stepping stone on an employee's journey toward their very different passion is a costly hire and makes for a bad investment. Asking the right questions is key: *What do you love about your chosen career? What courses in school did you dread? What inspires you?* You want to get a sense of who the person is and what they believe.

2. *Offer Safe and Open Communication*
    Once you hire the right people, you need to sit down regularly and discuss what is working well and what isn't. Evaluate the victories as well as the losses. A solid culture is one that identifies when things don't work and solves the problem. Also, people need to feel safe and trust they can speak freely without worrying about repercussions. Let them know they are valued and respected and that their ideas have merit.

3. *Cleanup Duty*
    A culture of passion can be altered by having the wrong people on board. One such element in an organization can be a whiner

or a complainer. These people usually don't address problems directly. They tend to gossip and complain and try to poison their coworkers' attitudes. These people are never an asset to an organization. Identify these people, and discuss with them their contributions to the company.

4. *Be Driven and Take Big Steps*
   Playing small never advances anyone or anything. You need a culture that supports big steps and powerful beliefs. "Make no little plans; they have no magic to stir men's blood." These words are attributed to Daniel Burnham, one of Chicago's most famous architects (quoted in Reardon 1992). Onward and upward should be the motto of any thriving enterprise. A city or company can be recreated after a fall or downturn. Don't let a temporary situation keep your thinking small.

5. *Welcome Differences*
   A staff of diverse backgrounds and experience allows for interesting interaction and debate. It also adds an interesting makeup to the group. The core values need to be in alignment with the company goals, but other differences can generate energy, which is critical to any enterprise.

6. *Create a Positive Physical Space*
   Take a look at your physical workspace. Is it set up in such a way to encourage interaction among the staff? Culture is made in the physical space. Can Engineering and Public Relations visit at the coffee machine? Would HR and Sales meet to visit in the break room? Look at your space and ask yourself, *Does this welcome interaction and connectivity?*

7. *Think Long-Term vs. Short-Term*
   Is the culture condemned for this quarter's earnings or the month's sales targets? If so, then could it be handicapped by short-term thinking? The culture needs to look ahead, not just in months, but in years or even decades. Work with your employees during the downturn to visit customers, target new markets,

and keep the momentum going. Don't pound on them for what may be a market condition rather than a real reflection on their efforts or ability. If there is a huge downturn in the market and the market is flat overall, encourage future growth and longer-term cycles. Lasting influence is better than a huge burst of sales. If you only keep track of the score and lose track of the ball, the game may not have a happy ending.

Hiring for, retaining, and developing your corporate culture is a skill all managers and senior executives need to learn. People work for more than just a paycheck these days. Employees who feel supported, heard, and cared about tend to work harder and stay with a company much longer. If you create a work culture of passionate employees, the company also gains a reputation as a fun place to work and attracts other, similar talent. Look at the success of Google and Microsoft. Their claim to fame is all about taking the time to hire the right fit for their companies' cultures. It yields great rewards.

CHAPTER 7
HUMAN TO HUMAN

Making a Better World

The steps of The Faremouth Method are a way to honor the fullness of what makes each human being unique. Whether one is a job seeker, a recruiter, or an employer, this work we do together to place people in jobs that fulfill them is not simply an economic task. It is where the personal becomes universal. When we make better matches, we create a stronger economy and a more stable workforce. This leads to fewer broken families, lower healthcare costs, and higher stability in our business world.

The old model of simply matching a resume to a job description—of matching one piece of paper to another—is how we lost the fine art required to help people into the jobs that mean the most to them. We are called now, by the downturn in our economy and the rapidly changing workforce, to learn the skill of matching the whole person to the job. Something changes in the human psyche when we reduce complex human beings, with their own hopes and dreams, to simple pieces of paper. We lose something of what binds us together as a human community.

Making a good match is critical for employers, recruiters, and applicants all over the globe. Happy, productive employees contribute to a thriving socioeconomic culture in a major way and have far-reaching effects on profitability, healthcare costs, and economic growth for a company. The right employee is a long-term investment that always pays off. We would all benefit from this revolutionary way of hiring, so we need to get on board now, embrace these new concepts, and begin spreading the word among our colleagues and peers. I practice The Faremouth Method for what I believe is the greater good. It's a technique that honors the complexity of being human and makes the world a better place.

How to Love Your Job

Loving what you do for a living begins with knowing who you are. When I traveled to Greece on a school trip with my younger son back in 2009, we visited the Temple of Apollo in Delphi. There, I saw a Greek inscription, the translation of which spoke to me: *know thyself*. It is said that, in ancient times, the Temple of Apollo emitted powerful vapors that gave the oracles amazing powers to make future predictions, and I truly felt a different type of energy there. In reflecting on this inscription, it hit me how profound the idea *know thyself* is for us as human beings. And as a recruiter, self-knowledge is critically important; we must know ourselves, our clients, and the folks we are hoping to place.

Knowing myself is vital to the job I perform daily. For me to make a good match of a candidate to a job, I have to dig deep, or "scrub down hard" as one client recently said in a testimonial, to find out who I am, who the client company is, who the candidate is, and how their passions and interests might align. If you do not know thyself and what your true skill set is, we must go on a mission to identify those qualities before we can make a good match.

Sometimes, self-knowledge comes easily. Other times, it takes months or even years to find the answer to the question *Who am I?* But when you know what you are passionate about, you can find a job that will align beautifully to those qualities. When you don't, you may go through many positions without finding where you are destined to be. As a job seeker, you must take the time to answer such a key question before you take the next job. It makes all the difference in finding a good fit and having a career you will enjoy for many years. It's crucial to your happiness—not only in finding a great job for yourself, but in finding out your true purpose and life destiny. This is how people come to love and feel a deep sense of loyalty to their jobs and to the companies they work for.

Live Life Creatively

Living a creative life sounds exciting, fun, and adventurous. But how do you get out of your comfort zone and move into something totally new? It's a scary thought for most people, especially since there is always a level of risk involved. But what is the old saying: "No guts, no glory"? If we stay in our comfort zones and never venture into something new, we never grow as human beings.

When I was in my early twenties, I had a secure job with a Big Three automaker working at their world headquarters. I had been there five years, had been promoted five times, and was the only female among thirty-seven engineers. My dad was so proud of me; he thought I should stay there and eventually retire from the company. He didn't take it too well when I told him I was leaving my secure job and moving to Houston to try my hand at my dream job. I had always wanted to be a recruiter, and back in the early eighties, the Big Three were having many struggles. Houston was "Boomtown," and this gal was ready to hop on the bandwagon and make it happen. I was lucky enough at the time to have a wonderful boss. When I went in and told him I was thinking of moving to Houston, he said, "Mary Ann, I think you should do it. You are a bright, hard-working young woman, and you don't want to wake up at forty years of age some day and say *What if?*" He told me to go and try my hand at my passion, and if it didn't work out, I could have my job back. I interviewed at many companies, received many offers, and finally decided to go to a small recruiting firm. After five months with the firm, I became one of the top-producing recruiters and was recruited away by a larger firm. My career had the same ups and downs as most young folks' when they are trying to find their life's work. But living my life creatively meant, to me, giving myself permission to make mistakes. It meant having people who believed in me and encouraged me to take risks.

As a young woman, I worked as a waitress. I had customers I loved and those who became friends and mentors to me, but many times I also had customers who tried my patience and tested my last nerve. But I always tried to keep my composure and make each of their meals seem like the most important part of my day. The skills I used as a waitress are some of the very same skills I use today. Of course, my job is much more complicated than serving hamburgers.

But I am still able to clearly see the association between the skills I used as a waitress and the skills I now use as a recruiter. And here I am, over thirty years later, still making placements. I can truly say I have lived life creatively. I love what I do, and I enjoy getting out of bed every morning and going to work. I have no regrets about living my life creatively. It's been a wonderful ride, and I wouldn't have had it any other way.

When searching for the right job for you, consider the experiences you may have had that align with your passions and skills. This inventory could give you some important information about the type of person you are and what skills you possess that might transfer into a career you love. To live a creative life, you must be willing to reinvent your life or change it when the path you're on is no longer taking you where you need to go.

Sometimes Last Becomes First

Years ago, I was in a sales seminar presented by Zig Ziglar. Zig was a phenomenal sales trainer, and I learned much from him. He told us something that stuck with me and became one of my strictest rules: "You can get everything in life you want if you will just help enough other people get what they want" (quoted in Eha 2012). Essentially, this told me that I should put myself last in the process of what I do. I learned not to let the fee I make become the determining factor of who I place and with whom.

The Faremouth Method isn't about greed and high production, though I have enjoyed a lucrative career because of the volume of placements that have come from it. But unlike some other practices I have observed, when I see an outstanding applicant with strong skills and experience, I don't rush the process and push them into a position just to make a big fee. I take the time to get to know the applicant, their needs, and their important requirements and try to align them with a job that fits those needs. Of course, there are many automated programs that can assist with the process of assessing a person's personality, needs, career expectations, etc. And in this world of high technology, those programs can be valuable tools.

I also use the same "Zig Ziglar" philosophy with client companies. If I have a client with a laundry list of expectations for a job and some turn out to be trainable, I explain to the employer how they might benefit from considering an alternative type of applicant. If they are looking for a sales assistant to assist technical sales people in the oil and gas market and the market is in a down cycle, allowing them time to train, someone who has worked as a sales assistant for a brokerage / financial company but wants to learn the oil and gas business could be easily trained to do this job. They have what are called *transferrable skills*.

The Five Gifts of Failure

It's been almost thirty years, but I clearly remember something a close relative said to me when my husband was about to try a new venture: "What if he fails?" I had thought it was an odd thing to say, but as a newly married woman, I replied, "Well if he fails, he will have learned something." My response was unusual for the time, but even to this day, that limiting belief system still haunts our society and so many people are terrified of failure. I've had my own share of failures, but I have learned more from them than from any of my successes.

The challenge of finding a job in today's market, and the many layoffs that have ensued from recent downsizing, can leave a person full of despair. But just because you experience a career failure doesn't mean you are doomed and your resume is toast. Despite the disappointment and embarrassment, a career failure can give you a running head start for the future. The next time you have dinner with an old friend who has just had their third promotion and wants to know how your life is going, keep your attitude positive and remember these five vital lessons that failure can offer:

I. *You know yourself better and are more in touch with important priorities.*
A career failure—whether a layoff, cutback, or termination—forces you to look deep within and examine what makes you

happy. After you get over the shock of the situation, you will likely experience relief and find yourself refocusing your goals in a new direction. It can almost be compared to having a new lease on life.

2. *Experience is your best teacher.*
   Coping with the unexpected is something you need to learn the hard way sometimes. The lessons you learn from major career setbacks can help you recognize warning signs that allow you to make better strategic decisions in the future. Being able to do an honest assessment of what fulfills you in a job can allow you to grow and develop in ways you never thought possible.

3. *You are able to widen your circle of coworkers and develop new friendships.*
   Changing jobs forces you to surround yourself with new people and energy. When we are surrounded by the same people day in and day out, we tend to not branch out with new experiences and adventures. New people in our circles can allow us to learn new hobbies and skills and develop ourselves in a way that makes us more interesting human beings.

4. *You become a more resilient human being and can better handle setbacks.*
   Bouncing back after a setback takes courage and determination. But it's only from the setbacks in life that we find out who we are and learn to handle challenges in our life with grace and poise. If you have been in the same job for twenty years and something happens, you tend to panic and freeze. If you have had setbacks in the past and lived through them, then you are better able to handle the unexpected and can instead grow from the experience.

5. *Your failures allow you to have more compassion and understanding for others.*
   Wisdom doesn't just materialize in a person. It takes painful experiences in many cases to be able to have empathy and compassion for others. Arrogance and insensitivity to the pain of

others are not admirable traits. Being humble, caring, and able to relate to friends and family who are going through tough times are traits that make us more attractive and real. The know-it-all who has never experienced challenge is probably not fun to be around for long.

If you follow failure instead of running from it, it might take you to exactly where you need to be. Sometimes, if you're lucky, you'll even realize that failure is the best thing that could have happened to you, providing you with the knowledge to do things you never thought you could.

What Do You Want Your Legacy to Be?

A recent survey of millennials asked what they thought would make them happiest. Of those interviewed, over 80 percent said *money*, while 50 percent of that same group said *fame*. But how does that compare with the mindset of older generations?

A study conducted by Harvard University, dubbed the "longest study on happiness," was presented in a 2015 TED Talk by the study's current director, Robert Waldinger (2015). As of the presentation, the study had followed a varied group of over seven hundred men for the last seventy-five years, sixty of which still lived.

The results? The common denominator of the subjects' happiness and healthiness (or lack thereof) turned out to be the positivity and support of their *relationships*.

Isn't life really about relationships? Whether you are a job seeker, employer, or recruiter, doesn't relating to or assisting another person bring on those *Ah Ha!* moments? At the end of your life, when your obituary is written, what do you want people to remember about you? Will it be the size of your home, the car you drove, the clothes you wore, the jewelry you owned, the trips you took, etc.? Or will it be about how your life may have helped another? I tell my kids all the time that, at my funeral, I hope someone will speak about how I helped others become the best versions of themselves. Or maybe I encouraged them at some point to try to become better or expand their careers. In many ways, our jobs define who we are. But for me, greed, fame, or living in a castle or mansion hasn't been high on my list of priorities. I enjoy getting up every morning and going into work because of the mental challenge of what I do and the personal fulfillment I get from helping others. One of my professors once told me, "Mary Ann, you have a good product; you just have to believe in it!" And I hope, as an executive recruiter, that is what I do for my applicants; I encourage them to look at their personal product, believe in it, and allow themselves to use those gifts and talents to contribute to the world.

When you are happy with you, the world becomes a better place. Your happiness radiates out into the world, and others can feel it. But it all starts with making a better you. Love yourself, honor your God-given gifts and talents, and use them in a way that allows you to make some type of contribution. We are all connected, and we can make a real difference—one small step at a time, one small accomplishment at a time, until the end of our lives. Do your own self-inventory; consider what you want your legacy to be. You have one life; make sure it's one you can be proud of.

Acknowledgments

I have been blessed in life to have so many people to thank for their assistance in this project. My late husband, Bob Sandland, inspired me more than I can ever describe. My wonderful parents, Florence and Frank Faremouth, taught me about hard work and how much it means to love what you do. My grandparents, Papa and Mimi, taught me how to help others, and their strong love of family and good food nourishes my soul to this day. My sons, Daniel and Christopher, always make me proud, and their wives, Valerie and Sara, are the daughters I never had. And my mother- and father-in-law, Nancy and Bill Sandland, have been so supportive through everything. I'm grateful to my sister, Lisa Faremouth-Weber, and her wonderful family, as well as Jack and Linda Ruffing, who have helped me more than they will ever know. My childhood friend, Linda States, and our many long talks on her porch will never be forgotten, nor will all the many family and friends who have been there along the way to cheer me on. Frank's Grill, my father's restaurant, taught me about customer service and how important it is to give more than you take. Thank you to all the wonderful folks at Toastmasters International, including Carol Carroway, Robert Bailey, and so many others. The thousands of applicants I have placed and companies who believed in my services are too many to mention. A special thanks goes to Joel Johnson, Margarita Torrente, and Natalia Johnson for all their hard work. I am grateful to the Sandland clan for being there through it all, and to Hailley and Hunter, my yellow labs, who showed so much affection through this interesting journey. My gratitude also goes to Marva Mason, my dearest friend, who met me at the ripe age of twenty-six and has always been a true friend. Her brilliant mind has always been a blessing to have in my world.

I am grateful to Mark Gelotte, the book designer who created my cover and designed the interior of this book; to Max Regan, my developmental editor and writing coach; and to Dorothy Tinker, my amazing copyeditor. My thanks goes out to Ford Motor Company for five wonderful years of the corporate world; to *Jobs: Houston*, the publication I owned for seven years, and the sixteen wonderful employees who helped make the magazine great; to Kathy McKree and HIPC for allowing me to serve as president and to work with amazing, talented women; and to the NASPD and NAPCA organizations, which have allowed me to form long-lasting relationships and continue to expand in my career.

And last, but not least, I give thanks to Almighty God, who is there for me no matter what and has always given me the strength and perseverance to climb every mountain, handle every challenge, and always continue to work for the greater good.

Mary Ann Faremouth is the founder and CEO of Faremouth & Company and a highly regarded speaker and writer. She has been a placement specialist and a leader in the national recruiting community since 1982. She is the 2016 president of the Houston Independent Personnel Consultant Group and is a member of the NASPD (National Association of Steel Pipe Distributors), the NAPCA (National Association of Pipe Coating Applicants), and the NAPC (National Association of Personnel Consultants). Her articles can be found in various industry-related publications. She cofounded *Jobs: Houston* magazine in 1997, one of the most popular employment magazines in Texas for over seven years. Mary Ann holds a CPC (Certified Personnel Consultant) credential, was certified by the Board of Regents of the National Association of Personnel Consultants in Washington, DC, and was recently awarded a Competent Communicator Award by Toastmasters. She maintains affiliations with professional organizations in various other industries, including oil and gas, financial, construction, IT, and structural, mechanical, and civil engineering. She has a keen understanding of the marketplace and its specialized needs and requirements. Mary Ann lives in Houston, Texas.

REFERENCES

Beyond. November 2011. "77% of Job Seekers Use Mobile Job Search Apps." *Beyond.* http://about.beyond.com/infographics/mobile-job-search-apps.

CareerBuilder. August 18, 2011. "Seventy-One Percent of Employers Say They Value Emotional Intelligence over IQ, According to CareerBuilder Survey," press release. http://www.careerbuilder.com/share/aboutus/pressreleasesdetail.aspx?id=pr652&sd=8%2f18%2f2011&ed=8%2f18%2f2099.

Deloitte. 2016. *The 2016 Deloitte Millennial Survey.* London: Deloitte. Accessed February 13, 2017. https://www2.deloitte.com/content/dam/Deloitte/global/Documents/About-Deloitte/gx-millenial-survey-2016-exec-summary.pdf.

Duckworth, Angela. 2016. *Grit: The Power of Passion and Perseverance.* New York: Scribner. Kindle edition.

Eha, Brian Patrick. November 30, 2012. "Zig Ziglar and the Importance of Helping Others." Entrepreneur. https://www.entrepreneur.com/article/225131.

Ferguson, Matt, Lorin M. Hitt, and Prasanna Tambe. 2013. *The Talent Equation: Big Data Lessons for Navigating the Skills Gap and Building a Competitive Workforce.* Columbus, OH: McGraw-Hill. Kindle edition.

Fernández-Aráoz, Claudio. June 27, 2014. "Is Your Company Ready for the Looming Talent Drought?" *Harvard Business Review.* https://hbr.org/2014/06/is-your-company-ready-for-the-looming-talent-drought.

Fortune. 2016. "Best Companies to Work For." *Fortune* magazine. Accessed February 13, 2017. http://fortune.com/best-companies.

Grant, Adam M. 2014. *Give and Take: Why Helping Others Drives Our Success.* New York: Penguin.

Hill, Napoleon. 2012. *Think and Grow Rich*. New York: Start Publishing. Kindle edition.

Jackson, Henry G. November 2014. "The Role of HR in Addressing the Challenges of an Aging Workforce." *HR Magazine* 59 (11): 1–3.

K@W. February 29, 2012. "Why the Job Search Is Like 'Throwing Paper Airplanes into the Galaxy.'" *Knowledge@Wharton*. http://knowledge. wharton.upenn.edu/article/why-the-job-search-is-like-throwing-paper-airplanes-into-the-galaxy/.

Kaslow, Amy. July 2012. "8 Steps for Closing the Skills Gap." AmyKaslow.com. Accessed February 13, 2017. http://www.amykaslow. com/8-steps-for-closing-the-skills-gap.

Leopold, Till Alexander, Vesselina Ratcheva, and Saadia Zahidi. January 2016. *The Future of Jobs: Employment, Skills and Workforce Strategy for the Fourth Industrial Revolution*. Geneva: World Economic Forum. Accessed February 8, 2017. http://www3.weforum. org/docs/WEF_Future_of_Jobs.pdf.

Marshall, Tess. 2011. "21 Tips to Release Self-Neglect and Love Yourself in Action." *Tiny Buddha: Simple Wisdom for Complex Lives*. http:// tinybuddha.com/blog/21-tips-to-release-self-neglect-and-love-your-self-in-action/.

"MBTI Basics," The Myers & Briggs Foundation, accessed February 7, 2017, http://www.myersbriggs.org/my-mbti-personality-type/mbti-basics.

McKale, Lisa. February 25, 2016. "Putting People Ahead of Profits: How to Improve Your Company's Culture." *Progressive Women's Leadership*. https://www.progressivewomensleadership.com/ putting-people-ahead-of-profits-how-to-improve-your-company-culture.

McLeod, Saul. 2007 (updated 2016). "Maslow's Hierarchy of Needs." *Simply Psychology*. http://www.simplypsychology.org/maslow.html.

Murphy, Mark. 2011. *Hiring for Attitude: A Revolutionary Approach to Recruiting and Selecting People with Both Tremendous Skills and Superb Attitude*. Columbus, OH: McGraw-Hill.

Pavlou, Christina. "How to Spot a Good Recruiter." *Workable*. Accessed March 1, 2017, https://resources.workable.com/tutorial/good-recruiter.

PwC. 2014. *17th Annual Global CEO Survey, 2014: US Report*. London: PricewaterhouseCoopers. Accessed February 8, 2017. http://www.pwc.com/us/en/ceo-survey-us/2014/assets/2014-us-ceo-survey.pdf.

Reardon, Patrick T. January 1, 1992. "Burnham Quote: Well, It May Be." *Chicago Tribune*. http://articles.chicagotribune.com/1992-01-01/news/9201010041_1_sentences-chicago-architects.

Safian, Robert. January 9, 2017. "How to Lead in 2017." *Fast Company*. https://www.fastcompany.com/3066307/work-smart/how-to-lead-in-2017.

Smith, Emily Esfahani, and Jennifer Aaker. December 30, 2016. "In 2017, Pursue Meaning Instead of Happiness." *Science of Us*. http://nymag.com/scienceofus/2016/12/in-2017-pursue-meaning-instead-of-happiness.html.

Sorenson, Susan. June 20, 2013. "How Employee Engagement Drives Growth." *Gallup Business Journal*. http://www.gallup.com/business-journal/163130/employee-engagement-drives-growth.aspx.

Vinod. January 1, 2015. "Life Begins at the End of Your Comfort Zone." *Life Probabilities* (blog). http://www.lifeprobabilities.com/2015/01/01/life-begins-at-the-end-of-your-comfort-zone.

Waldinger, Robert. November 2015. "What Makes a Good Life? Lessons from the Longest Study on Happiness" (presentation). *TED Talks*. http://www.ted.com/talks/robert_waldinger_what_makes_a_good_life_lessons_from_the_longest_study_on_happiness/transcript?language=en.

Wheeler, Kevin. March 22, 2011. "4 Traits that Separate a Great Recruiter from a Good One." *ERE Media*. https://www.eremedia.com/ere/4-traits-that-separate-a-great-recruiter-from-a-good-one.

Wood, Stephanie. December 25, 2014. "Answer 6 Questions to Reveal Your Life Purpose." *Success*. http://www.success.com/article/answer-6-questions-to-reveal-your-life-purpose.

Made in the USA
Middletown, DE
23 December 2021

56225212R00096